THE
STUDENT
VEGETARIAN
COOK
BOOK

First published in Great Britain in 1992
by Collins & Brown Limited
Letts of London House
Great Eastern Wharf
Parkgate Road
London SW11 4NQ

British Library Cataloguing-in-Publication Data:
A catalogue record for this book
is available from the British Library.

ISBN 1 85585 140 7

5 7 9 10 8 6 4

Conceived, edited and designed by Collins & Brown Limited

Editorial Director: Gabrielle Townsend

Editors: Sarah Bloxham and Ruth Baldwin

Art Director: Roger Bristow

Designed by: Claire Graham

Filmset by Goodfellow & Egan, Cambridge
Printed and bound in Finland by WSOY

THE
STUDENT
VEGETARIAN
COOK
BOOK

Eating well without meat,
mixer, microwave or money

Sarah Freeman

COLLINS & BROWN

• ACKNOWLEDGEMENTS •

A LOT OF people have helped with this book in one way or another and I am very grateful to them all. Those to whom I owe most, however, are the team of students who tested all the recipes promptly and with humour but in a truly critical spirit. The team was headed and organised by Polly Freeman; other members were Rob Kenney, Helen Leech, Danielle Power and Louise Simpson. Other testers were Julia Mitchell, Synda Younson and in particular Alex Freeman, who not only tested but also retested recipes, often many times, with patience, accuracy and remarkable flair: without him, a number would not have been included.

I also want to thank Jill Norman, author of The Complete Book of Spices, Clara Tomasi, formerly of Frith's Restaurant and who now runs Turnaround Cooks, Piero and Henrietta Amodio of the Coffee Gallery and Mauro of Mauro's Delicatessen for contributing recipes; the Milk and Potato Marketing Boards and Marks & Spencer PLC for information; the Ministry of Agriculture, Fisheries and Food, who kindly donated their latest publications on nutrition; my publishers for invaluable editorial advice and assistance, notably Sarah Bloxham and Ruth Baldwin, who have made every stage in the production of this book a pleasure; and last but most rather than least, my husband Michael, who has eaten his way through it despite not being a vegetarian and unfailingly commented constructively, besides giving positive help in very many other ways.

·CONTENTS·

INTRODUCTION

• IMPORTANT: PLEASE READ THIS •

Please read this (I have made it as short as possible) because it not only tells you about the book and the recipes but also includes practical information about equipment, ingredients, the storage of food and – most important of all – nutrition.

• THE BOOK •

The idea of the first *Student Cook Book* came from a group of students who wanted to be able to cook really good meals despite lack of time, money and experience; a team of them also tested and approved every recipe. Although many of the dishes did not include meat, partly for the sake of economy, it was not a book specifically for vegetarians. Since then, so many people have become vegetarian that the carnivorous recipes in it now seem a waste of space. I want to stress, however, that while this book is strictly vegetarian, all the recipes it contains have not only been tested by students as before but tasted and judged on the same basis as other dishes by non-vegetarians too, so that it is just as much for people who simply want to eat less meat as for those who are completely committed to vegetarianism.

If, when you look through the book, some of the recipes seem to you rather long, it is because of the needs of those with little cooking experience: I have taken nothing for granted but explained every process in detail, including how to prepare all the vegetables. In fact, most of the dishes are quite simple. The only ones which are more demanding are in the chapter on parties, where I felt that something a little different was needed.

• THE RECIPES •

Except for those in the chapters on bread and cakes and on giving parties, plus one or two for side salads or vegetable dishes, all the recipes are suitable for main courses. To simplify cooking and to save time, almost all of them are also of the one-dish-per-meal type. For reasons of time and economy, and also health, nobody wanted recipes for puddings, although two or three of a relatively healthy kind have slipped into the party section. Similarly I have given only a few recipes for cakes (but ensured that the few included are absolutely worth the occasional lapse of principle).

• EQUIPMENT •

Apart from a cooker, I have assumed that you will have the following: a wok or frying-pan, saucepans, colander, sieve, bowls, scales, and – I am afraid, since it is less obviously a necessity, and is expensive – a pestle and mortar. Whenever other items, such as ovenware dishes, baking-sheets or sauce-pans with lids are needed, I have listed them with the ingredients to enable you to borrow them if necessary. I have included saucepans with lids on this list because yours may not have them. Since a covered pan is essential for cooking rice and almost essential for simmering pulses, this is one item which is well worth buying if you can.

An alternative, which will probably be cheaper and will serve as both saucepan and frying-pan, is a wok with a lid – prefer-ably non-stick: if I had to manage with only one pan, I would choose this.

Sometimes lack of equipment can be overcome. You can use a beer or milk bottle instead of a rolling-pin, and packet sizes or tablespoons to replace scales. For example:

1 tablespoon sugar or 2 level tablespoons flour = 1 oz/25 g.
Similarly a milk bottle or mug can be used as a measuring-jug:

1 average-sized mug of liquid = ½ pint/300 ml.

I have given much thought to the question of pestles and mortars, and even offered a prize to anyone who could think of a cheap, efficient substitute, but without result. You can chop or crush nuts and/or garlic with the end of a rolling-pin (if you have one), but, aside from a grinder, there is no other way of pulverising spices. My only suggestion is that if you cannot afford a pestle and mortar yourself, you persuade somebody to give you one.

I have allowed for inaccurate ovens by excluding any recipe for which a very precise heat is needed, but in general if you think that your oven overheats (and it is not fan-operated), place items near the bottom; conversely, if it seems too cool, put them near the top (oven thermometers can be bought for a few pounds). I have no remedy for ovens which burn at the back except to advise turning items round during cooking.

• INGREDIENTS •

To avoid the need for excessive cross-referencing, I have discussed ingredients with the recipes, and want to make only a few general comments here. The most important is on freshness: this applies not only to vegetables but also to herbs and spices. Throughout the book I have taken fresh vegetables for granted except here and there where frozen peas or spinach, or (in only one instance) tinned tomatoes are an acceptable substitute. I know that tinned tomatoes save money as well as time, and also acknowledge that fresh ones seldom have much taste – but I still recommend them, if only because much of the vitamin content of the tinned ones will have been lost. I am also aware that fresh herbs may be difficult to buy and are expensive. Dried ones, however, cannot be used for salads and give nothing like the same flavour in cooking; the only exception here is dried oregano, which I have used in several recipes. The answer is to grow your own herbs. You can buy sets of seeds quite cheaply, or purchase plants in pots for the cost of two or three packets of cut herbs in a supermarket. The ones most often needed for the recipes are: parsley, chives, basil and dill; coriander, if you like it, is also useful. The first two grow easily; basil needs protection from cold and, as an annual, will not survive the winter, but will last throughout the summer on a sunny window-sill. The only one which presents a problem is dill, chiefly because it is a fairly large plant, but you could begin to pick and use it before it reached its full height.

Just as dried herbs give relatively little flavour, so do ready-ground as opposed to freshly crushed spices. As fresh toasting also contributes enormously to flavour, a home-prepared spice mixture such as curry powder has far more potency and character than the average equivalent that you can buy. I have

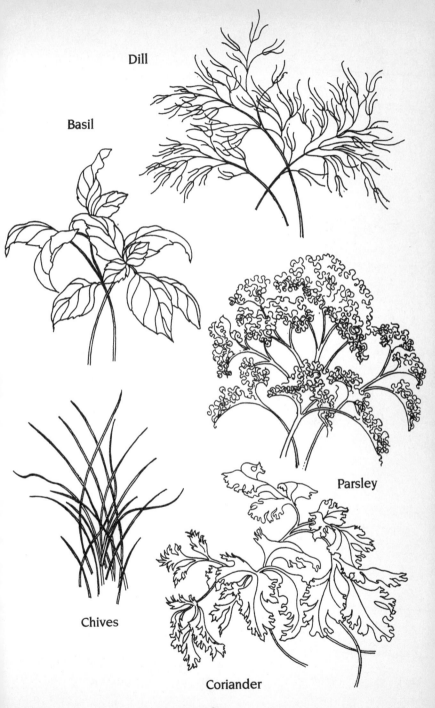

Dill

Basil

Parsley

Chives

Coriander

9

therefore suggested using freshly crushed spices and home-made mixtures throughout the book. In the same way, if you have a pepper mill or are prepared to crush your own pepper-corns, freshly ground pepper will make a difference to every dish. If you do use ready-ground pepper, choose black rather than white. Your cooking will also be transformed by the use of sea-salt instead of ordinary table-salt. In this instance, if you have no mill, use Maldon salt flakes (from supermarkets) which simply need roughly crushing with the back of a spoon.

The spices most often needed for the recipes are: coriander and cumin seeds, nutmegs and cinnamon sticks; for curries and an aromatic mixture known as garam masala you will also need poppy, mustard and fenugreek seeds, cardamom pods and ground asafoetida and turmeric. All are relatively cheap and can be bought at supermarkets, good grocers or health-food shops.

Another point is that fresh green chillies in particular vary considerably in strength. I have used chillies in many recipes not for heat but merely to provide an interesting undertone; an alternative might have been stock. Where heat is needed, however, I have been cautious: if you like hot flavours, you may wish to add an extra chilli. The only reliable guidance on strength I can offer is that one variety, which is roundish and crinkled and known as Scotch Bonnet is distinctly fierier than the rest. You should also note that the chemical which makes chillies hot may cause your hands to smart severely: in the recipes I have therefore suggested washing your hands after preparing them or wearing polythene gloves (available from supermarkets). The heat will also be transferred to the knife used for chopping and any food they may touch. Dried red ones affect the skin less but it is still wise to take precautions.

I have assumed that you will use plain dried beans; tinned ones are soggier but save soaking time.

• NUTRITION •

In composing and selecting the recipes which follow, my first consideration has been aesthetic – that is, taste. Next, however, has come health. As little oil as is consistent with good eating and culinary needs has been used, and vegetable oil and margarine rather than butter (which is a saturated fat) specified except where the taste of the butter really counts. Apart from a pastry recipe and a dip which calls for sour cream, I have avoided cream, and have given a recipe for a substitute (see page 180). Wholemeal flour and brown rice, which provide fibre and have a much higher vitamin and mineral content than their white counterparts, have been taken for granted throughout, although in one or two instances I have suggested white, or a proportion of white, for particular reasons. Pasta presents the dilemma that if on occasion you want to serve the fresh rather than the dried variety, you will have to use white because brown is almost unobtainable. I also happen to think that flour-based sauces flavoured with cheese, such as are used for lasagne and cannelloni, are better made with white flour because it gives a smoother, creamier consistency and brown masks the taste of the cheese; however, I have left this to you.

The claim that all the recipes can be eaten as main courses is justified not only by their nature but also by the fact that all except one (Guacamole) contain or are served with at least one high-protein ingredient. According to recent calculations, you need to eat an average of at least 1⅓–1⅔ oz/37–46 g of protein a day: this is easily achieved and you probably exceed it most of the time anyway, but all the same it should be borne in mind when planning meals. The most concentrated sources of protein are cheese and most nuts, seeds (especially sunflower seeds) and kidney beans, followed by other pulses, wheat and its products, and eggs. Vegetables (except peas and spinach) contain little, which means that a stir-fried dish of only vegetables or a meal of carrots and mashed potatoes will not give you all the kinds of nourishment you need. Also, because plant proteins (with the exception of soya) are of less value than animal ones if taken singly, more than one kind should be eaten at once. As a practical illustration, a day's quota might be 2 oz/50 g cheese, 2 oz/50 g peanuts, 3½ oz/100 g lentils and 2–5 slices of bread, some of which should be eaten at the same time as the lentils. Details of other nutritional needs and a table of food values are given on page 184, so I shall only draw attention to a few particular facts here: that chestnuts and coconuts contain very little protein, avocado pears not much more and rice significantly less than wheat; that spinach has more than other leaf vegetables and is also rich in iron, calcium and vitamins A and C; and that watercress, green peppers and strawberries are especially rich in vitamin C.

I should make it clear that while the needs of vegans have been considered and many of the recipes are suitable or can be adapted for them, this book has not been designed for them. In particular, I have included tofu only for gastronomic reasons and, apart from soy sauce, ignored other soya and similar products.

• STORAGE AND HYGIENE •

All dairy products except eggs should be placed in the refrigerator as soon as possible after purchase. Do not carry them around all day but shop on the way home. Most vegetables should also be stored in the refrigerator: the main exceptions are garlic, onions and most potatoes, which should be kept in a brown paper bag in a cool place out of the sun (very tiny new potatoes, if to be stored for any length of time, should go into the refrigerator). Bright light may cause potatoes of any age to develop poisonous green patches, which should be cut off before cooking. If your refrigerator is small, cabbages, carrots, parsnips and courgettes will stay firm and fresh outside it for one to several days according to room temperature. Eggs should not be chilled but kept cool.

Everything stored in the refrigerator should be left in its packages or wrapped in foodwrap: uncovered items allow bacteria to circulate. Dairy products and cooked dishes should be stored at the top and raw vegetables and fruit near the bottom. Most vegetables will keep for 2 days or more; cooked dishes 1 day; yoghurt usually 1–2 days after its sell-by date. Cheese, especially soft cheese, should be eaten by or before its sell-by date. Keep a check on sell-by dates and clean out the refrigerator once a week.

Outside the refrigerator, potatoes will keep for 1–2 weeks according to room temperature; onions and garlic 3–4 weeks. Tomatoes, avocado pears and other fruit will ripen; eggs should be eaten by their sell-by date and as a general rule should be as fresh as possible. Dry groceries such as sugar, pulses, flour, rice, dried pasta, loose nuts, dried chillies and spices should be kept cool and dry; pulses, although they can be stored for some time, will cook more quickly if they are fresh. Spice mixtures should be kept in air-tight containers (freezer containers with sealed lids are ideal).

Organic produce will not keep as long as that grown by conventional methods. All vegetables are more nutritious and taste better the sooner they are eaten.

Wash your hands after preparing vegetables and handling raw eggs, before starting to cook, and in particular before kneading or mixing dough, rolling out pastry, shaping burgers or croquettes and preparing salads.

• PREPARATION AND COOKING •

Complete directions are given with every recipe except for these following general points:

To *chop onions* quickly and prevent them from rolling about, cut in half lengthways and place them cut-side down: they can then be sliced and cross-chopped without difficulty.

To *chop parsley* quickly, gather it into a tight bunch and cut fine slices across.

To *peel tomatoes*, cover with boiling water and leave for about 30 seconds; unless they are underripe, the skin will then peel off easily. If they are too hot to handle, plunge them into cold water for a few seconds before peeling.

Vegetables should be chopped just before you want to use them since they start to lose their vitamins as soon as they are cut. As vitamins will also escape into the cooking water, add only just enough to cover them and re-use it afterwards for simmering rice or boiling pasta. Meanness with water also carries the bonus that the less you use, the more flavour the vegetables will have.

To *simmer* means to cook in water which is just on the point of boiling: it moves on the surface or bubbles slightly but not vigorously. To achieve this you need to adjust the heat carefully; you also have to remember that if you add a lid, the temperature in the saucepan will rise slightly.

Eggs should be washed before cracking in case pieces of shell, which could cause contamination, fall into the contents. To crack cleanly, tap sharply on the edge of the bowl or pan.

·DIPS, PÂTÉS·
AND ZESTS

Dips and pâtés are always useful, not only when friends come round and at dinner-parties, but also for lunch or the odd snack: they are much healthier than biscuits or bread and jam and make a change from peanut butter. The virtues of peanut butter, however, have led me to include recipes for other sorts of nut butter, which are very easy to make and surprisingly delicious. I have also given a recipe for tomato jam, which is by far the most adaptable item in the book because you can use it to add interest to a variety of cooked dishes or, like pickle and chutney, in sandwiches.

Dips are much more interesting if, as well as bread, you serve them with a selection of crudités: that is, raw vegetables. Almost any vegetable which does not have to be cooked (as, for instance, potatoes do) is suitable provided that it is crisp and fresh. Besides the more obvious, such as cucumber, carrots, celery and peppers, you can use celeriac, turnips, mange-tout or sugar-snap peas and small string beans. To prepare cucumber and carrots, wash or scrub and dry them, cut off the ends and chop into sticks: the quickest way to do this is to slice them into 1–1½ inch/2.5–4 cm lengths and cross-chop. For celery, cut off the root ends and leaves, pare away any brown streaks, wash and dry; if the sticks are deeply curved, hold them under the cold tap to wash out dirt on the inside. Wash, dry and quarter peppers; remove the white inner membrane, the core and all the seeds (which are hot: hence the name), cut out any dark spots and slice. Peel celeriac (which has a slightly aniseed taste) and trim away any brown knots or fibres under the skin; chop into sticks and, since it may discolour on exposure to the air, sprinkle with a little lemon juice – which will also enhance its flavour. Peel and chop turnips. Wash cauliflower, pare off any trace of pink or brown mould and cut into narrow florets. Wash mange-tout or sugar-snap peas and trim the stalk ends. Wash beans and trim the ends.

Another alternative for serving with dips is rusks. These are simply bread baked in the oven until crisp all through. They are really a form of croûton but larger and cooked more slowly.

• RUSKS •

Use stale bread if possible (easier to cut tidily than fresh). Pre-heat the oven to 400°F, 200°C, Gas Mark 6. Cut the bread into slices of moderate thickness, discard the crusts and chop into wide fingers. Bake for 20 minutes or until slightly browned.

• GUACAMOLE •

I tried out all the dips and pâtés in this chapter (except Clara's Lentil and Lime Pâté) at a Christmas party and took the order in which they disappeared as a measure of their popularity. This won easily – but do not make it too often because avocados, although they contain a high proportion of oil, which is why they are so satisfying, are very low in protein.

It is important that you choose an avocado at the right stage of ripeness. The green ones are easy to judge: if they give slightly to the touch all over, they are ready to eat. Avoid any which are very soft or have squashy patches, as they will be overripe and streaked with black inside. Hard ones are under-ripe but if left at room temperature will soften in a few days. The almost-black variety is more of a problem because it has nubbly, relatively hard skin, but you can still tell if the flesh underneath is hard or soft.

Do not rub your eyes while handling the chilli and wash your hands immediately afterwards; if you have sensitive skin, wear polythene gloves while preparing it. *For 3–4.*

• INGREDIENTS •

½ *green chilli*

6 *spring onions*

1 *small clove garlic*

1 *large avocado*

1 *lemon*

Salt

Paprika

15

• METHOD •

1 Wash and dry the chilli. Trim off the stalk end, cut in half lengthways and discard the seeds. Cut out the white inner pith and dice the flesh as finely as possible. Wash your hands.

2 Trim and finely slice the onions. Peel and finely chop the garlic. Squeeze half the lemon.

3 Cut the avocado in half and ease out the stone (if you have space, plant it: it is easily grown and becomes an attractive houseplant). Mash the flesh with a fork. Add and stir in the prepared ingredients with a moderate pinch of salt and a little paprika. Taste and add a little juice from the second half of the lemon and more salt or paprika as desired (quite a generous amount of salt is in fact needed, but it is wiser to add extra at the end than to put in too much before tasting).

• CLARA'S LENTIL • AND LIME PÂTÉ

This is much more pungent and rather dearer to make than Lentil and Lemon Pâté (see page 163), chiefly because of the limes – but their flavour, and in particular the aromatic zest, justifies the extra cost. This pâté also contains chillies, but does not strike one as hot: they simply add depth to the flavour.

Clara is Clara Tomasi, a top Italian chef who for some years owned a restaurant in London's Soho called Frith's where all the ingredients used were organic and vegetarian cooking a speciality. My first thought when I was asked to write this book was that I simply must include several of the dishes I had eaten there: Clara has given me not only this recipe but also one or two others, and has demonstrated her way of making polenta (see page 128).

Her original ingredients for the following included 6 table-spoons of extra virgin (the best) olive oil and Puy lentils: I have economised on the oil and suggest using brown lentils, since the Puy variety, which are small and black and considered very superior, are fairly difficult to buy. Red onions are milder than the usual white ones (see also Greek Salad, page 114).

Half the lentils are mashed to a pâté-like consistency and half left whole to match the other ingredients in texture.

Serve the pâté with rusks (see page 15 for how to make your own), warm pitta or firm white bread (such as Italian Pugliese). For 4.

• INGREDIENTS •

2 *cloves garlic*	4 *limes*
5 *oz/150 g brown lentils*	3 *green chillies*
Salt	About 2 *tablespoons olive oil*
1 *small red onion*	Pepper

Saucepan with a lid

• METHOD •

1 Peel and finely chop the garlic. Pick over and rinse the lentils. Put both into the saucepan with a lid. Add 1 pint/600 ml water (but no salt), bring to the boil and boil briskly for 2 minutes. Reduce the heat, cover and simmer for 25 minutes. Add a little salt and, if the lentils are dry, 3 fl oz/75 ml or less boiling water: it is important not to add much because when cooked they should be quite dry. Continue simmering for 5–10 minutes more or until they are tender when prodded with a fork.

2 Peel and finely chop the onion. Wash and dry the limes. Finely grate the zest and add to the onion; squeeze the juice and pour it into a cup. Wash and dry the chillies; cut off the stalk ends, slit in half and discard the seeds and white inner pith. Chop as finely as possible; do not rub your eyes while handling them, and wash your hands immediately afterwards. Add the chopped chillies to the onion and lime zest.

3 Put about half the cooked, dry lentils into a bowl and mash with a fork. When fairly smooth, return them to the rest in the saucepan and heat briefly, stirring continuously (this is because they should be hot when the rest of the ingredients are added). Remove from the heat and stir in the oil, the chilli, onion and lime zest mixture, a generous sprinkling of pepper, just under

½ teaspoon salt and most of the lime juice. Mix, then add the rest of the juice gradually: if the lentils were dry, they should absorb all of it, but it is better to use a little less than make the pâté too liquid. If it still seems dry when all the juice is added, pour in a little more oil. Leave to cool, taste and adjust the seasoning if necessary.

•CHEESE AND CHILLI DIP•

This makes a tasty sandwich filling as well as an excellent dip: either way, accompany it with wholemeal bread and any kind of crisp salad vegetable. When Cheddar cheese is neeeded for flavouring, it really does pay to use a strong, mature type even though it costs a little extra (best of all, but still more expensive, is mature farmhouse-made Cheddar). *For* 3–4.

•INGREDIENTS•

6 *spring onions*	¼ *pint/142 ml sour cream*
½ *green chilli*	*Paprika*
2 *oz/50 g Parmesan and* 2 *oz/50 g Gruyère or* 4 *oz/125 g strong Cheddar cheese*	*Salt*

•METHOD•

1 Trim and finely chop the onions. Wash and dry the chilli and slit it in half lengthways; wrap the half not needed in foodwrap and store in the refrigerator. Trim the stalk from the half to be used, discard the seeds and white inner pith and chop the flesh as finely as you can. Do not rub your eyes while handling it and wash your hands directly afterwards.

2 Finely grate the cheese or cheeses (it will not mix smoothly with the cream if coarsely grated: for this reason do not use ready-grated Cheddar).

3 Mix the prepared ingredients with the sour cream, a fair pinch of paprika and a little salt; taste and add more seasoning if necessary.

•LOW-FAT COTTAGE•
CHEESE DIPS

It may seem silly to give recipes for cottage cheese when so many flavoured kinds can be bought, but (as with yoghurt) additions made at home are healthier and almost always taste better if only because they are fresher.

•COTTAGE CHEESE WITH•
APPLE AND CELERY

Whereas almost all kinds of fruit are delicious accompanied by cottage cheese (see page 117), only a few seem to me successful when mixed into it. One of these is apple, preferably with a stick of celery. For 8 oz/250 g cheese, you will need ½ crisp apple (such as Granny Smith) and a small, inner stick of celery. Trim the leaf and root end of the celery, wash, dry and chop very finely. Wash the apple, remove the core and chop the flesh fairly finely. Add to the cheese with ⅓ teaspoon salt.

•COTTAGE CHEESE•
WITH HERBS

I have tried various herbs and combinations of herbs at different times and have to report what everyone already knew: that one of the very best ways of flavouring cottage cheese is with chives. You need more chives than you might think – 1 heaped tablespoon (when chopped) for 8 oz/250 g cheese, which means quite a fat bunch. If the chives are bought rather than home-grown, pick them over, throwing away any brownish or floppy leaves. Trim the ends, wash, blot dry with kitchen paper and chop very finely. Add to the cheese with a moderate sprinkling of pepper and ⅓ teaspoon salt. (Do not add garlic.)

In a different way, dill works equally well. For 8 oz/250 g cottage cheese, you will need 1 dessertspoon (when chopped), which means 5–6 fair-sized spears. Wash, blot dry with kitchen paper and pull the leaves (which are like filaments) from the main stems. Chop very finely and add to the cheese with seasoning as above.

• COTTAGE CHEESE •
WITH WALNUTS

Adding walnuts means adding fat, but the result is too good not to mention. The effect almost depends, however, on crisping the nuts: the best method is to bake them in the oven, but if this means heating it specially, you may prefer to use a saucepan.

For baking, pre-heat the oven to 400°F, 200°C, Gas Mark 6. Cover a small baking-sheet with aluminium foil. For 8 oz/250 g cottage cheese, spread 2 oz/50 g walnut pieces over the foil and bake for 5 minutes. To toast the nuts in a saucepan, put them into a thick pan (dry-toasting will make it very hot) and set over high heat for 1½–2 minutes; shake constantly, since they burn very easily.

Allow to cool, chop roughly, then add to the cheese with ⅓ teaspoon salt and a moderate sprinkling of pepper.

• NUT BUTTERS •

The last thing I would wish is to discourage anyone from eating peanut butter – but still, everyone needs a change and other kinds of nut butter are less easy to buy and expensive. Unfortunately the cost of nuts justifies the price and means that the saving on making your own is insignificant; also, without a grinder, you cannot achieve the creamy smoothness of the commercial product. The crushed, home-made versions, however, really do taste infinitely better than the bought ones.

Of the kinds of nut I have tried (I excluded peanuts), I think that by far the best butter is made with almonds; next come hazelnuts, which are pleasant alone but also very good with spice; walnuts give the smoothest result but are slightly bitter.

The butters will keep for at least a week in the refrigerator. *Makes about 4 oz/125 g butter.*

• INGREDIENTS •

3½ oz/100 g almonds, hazelnuts *or walnuts*

About 2–2¼ tablespoons sunflower *or other light oil*

Salt

Small baking-sheet

• METHOD •

1 Pre-heat the oven to 400°F, 200°C, Gas Mark 6. Line the baking-sheet with aluminium foil and spread the nuts over it. Bake walnuts for 6–8 minutes, hazelnuts for 10–12 minutes and almonds for 14–16 minutes or (in all cases) until the nuts are lightly browned.

2 Crush the roasted nuts as finely as possible. Add a generous pinch of salt to walnuts, a moderate pinch to hazelnuts and very little or none to almonds. Mix with the oil; if you want a fairly liquid result, you may need to add a little extra.

• SPICED HAZELNUT BUTTER •

• INGREDIENTS •

3½ oz/100 g hazelnuts

Salt

2 teaspoons sesame seeds

2–2¼ tablespoons sunflower oil

1 teaspoon coriander seeds

Small baking-sheet

• METHOD •

Bake and crush the nuts as on page 21. Toast the sesame and coriander: put into a small saucepan over medium heat for 1–2 minutes or until they start to change colour, shaking constantly to ensure even cooking (beware of the sesame, which spits). Crush finely. Add a pinch of salt and mix with the nuts and oil.

• PETER GORDON'S • TOMATO JAM

Peter Gordon is a chef from New Zealand who worked with Clara Tomasi at Frith's Restaurant in London. This jam is a cross between ordinary jam and chutney: it is pungent rather than sweet but contains no vinegar. Like chutney, it goes with a wide variety of savoury dishes, such as burgers, pancakes and fritters (at Frith's I had it with plantain fritters), or can be used to flavour yoghurt or in sandwiches. If put into a sterilised jar, it will keep for months; but because it contains very little sugar, once opened it must be stored in the refrigerator and eaten within a few days. For this reason, if you have them, it is a good idea to put it into two small jars (6 oz/190 g in size, such as those in which peanut or other nut butters are sold) rather than one large one. However, as the jars should be full, do not be tempted to half-fill two larger ones. With fresh tomatoes, the quantities below will fill one 12 oz/375 g jar; with tinned, because of the size of the tins, there will be a little more.

Plum tomatoes, which are large and plum-shaped rather than round, give a much better result than ordinary round ones, which are too watery to produce a jam-like consistency; fresh plum ones are becoming easier to buy, although relatively expensive, but tinned ones are widely available. If the choice is between fresh ordinary and tinned plum tomatoes, I (for once) recommend tinned (but *not* tinned ordinary ones; you should also avoid chopped tinned plum ones flavoured with garlic).

Even using fresh tomatoes, the jam takes only a few minutes to prepare, but you need to allow 2¼–2½ hours for it to simmer. *Makes about* 12 oz/375 g.

• INGREDIENTS •

1½ lb/750 g fresh or
2 x 14 oz/ 400 g tins plum tomatoes

3–4 cloves garlic

1 fresh or dried red chilli

2 oz/50 g granulated sugar

Salt

• METHOD •

1 If using fresh plum tomatoes, peel and chop them, discarding the cores; if using tinned ones, chop them and discard the stalk ends. Peel and finely chop the garlic. Wash and dry the chilli, trim the stalk end, slit lengthways and remove the seeds; dice the flesh as finely as possible. Do not rub your eyes while handling it, especially if it is fresh, and wash your hands directly afterwards (or wear polythene gloves).

2 Put all the ingredients, including the juice from tinned tomatoes if using them, into a saucepan with a pinch of salt. Set over low heat, stirring occasionally, until the sugar has dissolved or the fresh tomatoes have run a couple of inches of juice; prod to submerge all the fruit, bring to the boil and simmer for 2¼–2½ hours or until the tomatoes are reduced to a thick, jam-like consistency and run no free liquid when stirred.

TO PRESERVE THE JAM

If you want the jam to keep, you will have to sterilise the jar(s). This is a bit of a bore but very easy. Start when the jam has been simmering for 2 hours.

**1 x 12 oz/375 g or 2 x 6 oz/190 g jars
with screw tops
Large saucepan
Small baking-sheet
2 oven-cloths or thick tea-cloths**

• METHOD •

1 Thoroughly wash the jar(s) and top(s) using detergent and rinse well. Place in the large saucepan and cover with water. Put a tablespoon inside each jar with the handle resting over the edge of the pan. Bring to the boil and boil briskly for at least 10 minutes.

2 Pre-heat the oven to 300°F, 150°C, Gas Mark 2, and line a small baking-sheet with aluminium foil. Up-end the jar(s) on the spoon(s), using a cloth as the handle(s) may be hot; drain out the water and set upside-down on the foil (use a second cloth to handle the jar(s) as it/they will be very hot: do not touch the inside). Fish out the top(s) with one of the spoons and place on the foil topside-up. Return the spoon to the water in the saucepan (there is no need to reboil it). Dry the jar(s) and top(s) in the oven for 10–15 minutes or until there is no moisture around them on the foil. Leave, without moving, to cool.

3 When the jam is ready, shake surplus water from the spoon and use it to put the jam into the jar(s). It/they should be filled to the neck. Screw on the top(s). Allow to cool and store in a cool cupboard. Allow any surplus jam to cool, cover and store in the refrigerator; eat promptly.

·SOUPS·

People tend to think of soups merely as the first course of a meal or as an alternative to sandwiches for lunch, but the soups in this chapter are quite as much meals in themselves as rice, pasta or other similar dishes. This is perhaps less true of Piero's Spinach Soup than of the others, but if you serve it with bread, preferably warmed in the oven, you will not need more than yoghurt or fruit afterwards. To combine proteins you should also serve bread with the bean soups, even though they are already substantial. All but the spinach soup, the flavour of which to some extent depends on Parmesan cheese, are suitable for vegans if they omit Parmesan for sprinkling or replace it with a suitable alternative.

Stock is helpful in making many soups but presents the problem that fresh vegetable stock means using and throwing away the vegetables, while the average stock cube gives a flavour which is often worse than none (there are one or two relatively good ones, but they are the exception). I have, however, suggested using a cube for Beetroot Soup, where it really cannot be tasted, and have given a basic stock recipe for Mock Minestrone which calls for only one carrot, one stick of celery and an onion; for the other soups, stock is not needed.

·BEETROOT SOUP·

This is not only thick and satisfying but, because of the deep red colour, remarkably picturesque: serve it with a generous sprinkling of chopped green parsley and a dollop of creamy yoghurt in each bowl. Its sole drawback is that the yoghurt is the only high-protein ingredient it contains, for which you should compensate by serving cheese afterwards or at another meal.

Buy raw rather than pre-cooked beetroot (which has probably been boiled with malt vinegar). Choose floury potatoes (Marfona, Pentland Dell, Pentland Squire or Maris Piper). For 4.

25

• INGREDIENTS •

1 lb/500 g raw beetroot

12 oz/375 g (2 medium) floury potatoes

2 vegetable stock cubes or sufficient to make up 2 pints/1 litre stock

1 large onion

3 cloves garlic

3–4 oz/90–125 g (1 large) carrot

2 oz/50 g (1 large stick) celery

Small bunch parsley

About 1 tablespoon oil

2 tablespoons tomato purée

4 slightly rounded teaspoons dark soft brown sugar

1 scant tablespoon red wine vinegar

Salt

Pepper

7 oz/200–225 g pot Greek or Greek-style yoghurt

Large saucepan

• METHOD •

1 Peel and slice the beetroot and potatoes; slice the beetroot very thinly (this makes it easier to mash). Make up the stock according to the instructions on the packet. Put the beetroot and potatoes into a saucepan with enough stock to cover them, setting any surplus aside. Bring to the boil and simmer for 30–40 minutes or until the beetroot is tender. Drain over a bowl to catch the cooking liquor and mash with a fork. To mash the beetroot thoroughly will take time: tackle it slice by slice.

2 Peel and finely chop the onion and garlic, keeping each separate. Peel and finely dice the carrot. Trim the root and leaf ends of the celery, pare off any brown streaks, wash and slice finely. Trim the parsley stalks, wash and leave to drain.

3 Put the onion into the large saucepan with the oil and fry over low heat, turning frequently, for 8–10 minutes or until soft and translucent but not brown. Add the garlic and fry for 4–5 minutes more, until the onion and garlic are just beginning to change colour. Add the carrot and celery and turn briefly in the oil, adding a little more if the pan is very dry. Pour in the beetroot/potato liquor and any remaining stock, bring to the boil and simmer for 15–20 minutes or until the carrot is tender.

4 Stir in the tomato purée, sugar, vinegar, mashed beetroot and potato, a light seasoning of salt and rather more pepper, and simmer for 20–25 minutes. Chop the parsley. Add more salt to the soup to taste (quite a lot is needed, but the stock may have been salty). Serve and add a blob of yoghurt in the centre of each bowl. Top with chopped parsley.

• PIERO'S SPINACH SOUP •

Piero runs a coffee-bar-cum-art-galley in London near the British Museum which is a popular meeting-place. As well as coffee and a small but luscious selection of cakes, he makes a few hot dishes for lunch. The recipes come from his mother, who lives in Amalfi, near Naples.

If real spinach is not available, a similar-looking vegetable with large, dark green leaves and thick, white stems is sometimes sold instead: this is sea-kale beet or Swiss chard. Another (although less common) alternative is New Zealand spinach, which has small, dark leaves growing from a central stem, rather like mint. Both (particularly New Zealand spinach) are good in their own right and sometimes an acceptable substitute for real spinach. In this soup, however, real (fresh) spinach makes the difference between a merely pleasant and a truly delicious result.

When possible, choose spinach pulled up by the roots, which will probably be in better condition than individual leaves. If you buy more than you need, pull off the roots, pick over and wash all of it and store the surplus in a food bag in the refrigerator: it will stay fresh for at least 2 days.

As potatoes are included in the recipe chiefly to absorb fat and thicken the soup, use floury ones (Marfona, Pentland Dell, Pentland Squire, Cara or Maris Piper). *For* 4.

• INGREDIENTS •

1 *lb*/500 *g spinach*	½ *tablespoon oil*
Salt	½ *oz*/15 *g butter*

1 *medium onion*	1 *teaspoon white flour*
3 *cloves garlic*	*Pepper*
1 *stick celery*	2 *oz/50 g Parmesan cheese*
8–10 *oz/250–310 g (2 medium or 1 large) floury potatoes*	1 *pint/600 ml milk*

Large saucepan with a lid

• METHOD •

1 Pull off the spinach roots and discard, together with any weeds or damaged leaves. Wash the spinach, twice if necessary. Put into the saucepan with ½ teaspoon salt and 1 tablespoon water (in theory no water is necessary, as it will cook in the residue left on the leaves after washing and, as it begins to cook, in its own juices, but I suggest adding a very little just in case). Cover and cook over medium heat for 5–6 minutes or until the spinach is tender and submerged in liquid. Drain in a colander set over a bowl to catch the liquid. Press out surplus moisture with the back of a spoon and chop finely. Measure the liquid and make up to 1 pint/600 ml with water.

2 Peel and finely chop the onion and garlic. Trim the root and leaf ends of the celery, pare off any brown streaks, wash and slice finely. Peel and thinly slice the potato(es).

3 Put the onion into the saucepan with the oil and butter and fry for 8–10 minutes, stirring often, until soft and translucent but not brown. Add the garlic and continue frying for 3–4 minutes; add the celery and fry for about another minute, turning continuously. Stir in the flour. Add the spinach liquid and potato slices, season with ½ teaspoon salt and a moderate sprinkling of pepper, bring to the boil and simmer for 20–25 minutes or until the potato is soft.

4 Grate the Parmesan. Add the milk to the soup, bring to the boil and simmer for 4–5 minutes. Stir in the spinach, bring to the boil again and remove from the heat. Stir in the cheese and serve.

• MOCK MINESTRONE •

This is not quite minestrone because, strictly speaking, minestrone should contain pasta or rice, which I have replaced with beans – not just on nutritional grounds but also for the sake of taste. It is very decidedly a meal in itself, the more so as it is better eaten on the day it is made. If it is kept, the vegetables become soggy and the flavour deteriorates.

It is the only recipe in the book for which I really do advise sacrificing a carrot, an onion and a stick of celery (which can be a tough, outside one) for stock. It takes very little time, since it can be simmered while the beans cook, and really does make all the difference to the finished soup.

• INGREDIENTS •

4 oz/125 g cannellini or haricot beans, soaked overnight in cold water

2 sticks celery

12 oz–1 lb/375–500 g leeks

4 oz/125 g cabbage

1 lb/500 g ripe tomatoes

4 oz/125 g mushrooms (preferably large)

1 largish onion

3–4 cloves garlic

1 teaspoon cumin seeds

1 fresh or dried red chilli

1 tablespoon olive oil

Pepper

2 tablespoons tomato purée

Parmesan to serve

STOCK

1 carrot

1 onion

1 outside stick celery

1 bayleaf

A few peppercorns

Salt

Saucepan with a lid
Large saucepan

• METHOD •

1 Drain the beans, rinse in cold water and put into the saucepan with a lid. Bring to the boil in 1 pint/600 ml water (do not add salt), skim and boil briskly for 5 minutes. Reduce the heat, cover and simmer for 40 minutes; add a little more water if necessary.

2 Make the stock. Peel and finely slice the carrot and onion. Trim the root and leaf ends from the celery, wash and slice finely. Bring the vegetables to the boil in 1½ pints/900 ml water with the bayleaf, 3 or 4 peppercorns and ½ teaspoon salt, reduce the heat, then simmer for 20 minutes. Strain and discard the vegetables.

3 Cut the leaf and root ends from the celery for the soup; wash and slice finely. Add with the stock to the beans when they have simmered for 40 minutes. Cover and continue to simmer for a further 5–10 minutes or until the beans are tender.

4 Chop the green leaf and root ends from the leeks, peel off the outer layer, wash and finely slice. Wash and shred the cabbage, cutting out any very thick stems. Peel and chop the tomatoes, throwing away the hard cores. Trim the mushroom stalks; peel, rinse and dry large ones or wash and dry small ones, chop into ½ inch/1 cm cubes or (if very small) slice fairly finely. Peel and finely chop the onion and garlic. Crush the cumin. Wash and dry the chilli, remove the stalk end and seeds, and dice the flesh as finely as possible. Do not rub your eyes while chopping it, particularly if it is fresh, and wash your hands directly afterwards (or wear polythene gloves).

5 Using the large saucepan, fry the onion in the oil over low heat, turning frequently, for 8–10 minutes or until soft and translucent but not brown. Add the garlic and fry for 3–4 minutes. Add the cumin and fry for 1–1½ minutes. Add the mushrooms, season moderately with pepper and more lightly with salt and continue frying gently, turning very often, for 5–7 minutes or until soft. Add the tomatoes, season very lightly and simmer for 7–10 minutes or until liquified, pressing out the lumps of flesh against the sides and bottom of the pan. Stir in the tomato purée. Add the leeks, cabbage and beans with the celery and stock. Cover and simmer for 40 minutes or until the leeks and cabbage are tender. Serve hot with crusty bread and plenty of grated Parmesan cheese.

•CLARA'S BEAN AND• BASIL SOUP

It is a bit unfair to include basil in the name of this soup, since the first time I made it I had no basil and it was still delicious. Sun-dried tomatoes are fast becoming more widely available and can now be bought at supermarkets as well as delicatessens and Italian grocers' shops. The same applies to pecorino cheese, similar to but cheaper than Parmesan and in my opinion often preferable; if there is a choice, the kind with the most positive, salty flavour is Roman pecorino.

If you cannot buy sun-dried tomatoes, black olives are an excellent subsitute. Black olives have been picked when the fruit is ripe, green when it is unripe: green are sharper. They may be preserved in oil, brine or vinegar: avoid those in vinegar. A possible replacement for basil is fresh or dried oregano.

The soup is simple to make and relatively inexpensive. Sun-dried tomatoes are quite expensive (especially those preserved in olive oil), but you don't need many, and you can also use them in the Cassoulet on page 102.

The flavour of the soup deteriorates if it is kept, so finish it on the day it is made. If there are only three of you, I suggest using only 6 oz/190 g beans: keep the quantities of the other ingredients as they are. *For* 4.

•INGREDIENTS•

8 oz/250 g cannellini or haricot beans, soaked overnight in cold water

1 medium onion

3 cloves garlic

Small handful parsley (enough for 1 heaped tablespoon when chopped)

1½ oz/40 g (6 halves) sun-dried tomatoes or 2 oz/50 g black olives

1 tablespoon olive oil

Salt

Pepper

8–10 *fresh basil or a handful*
fresh oregano leaves (enough for 1
  tablespoon when chopped) or 1
  rounded teaspoon dried oregano

2–3 *oz/50–90 g pecorino or*
3–4 *oz/90–125 g Parmesan cheese*

Saucepan with a lid

• METHOD •

1 Drain the beans, rinse in cold water and put into the saucepan with a lid. Add just over 2 pints/1 litre of cold water (but no salt). Bring to the boil, skim and boil briskly for 5 minutes. Reduce the heat, cover and simmer for 45–50 minutes or until the beans are tender when prodded with a fork. You will need to add more boiling water: keep an eye on them and, when the level is low, add 1¼ pints/750 ml.

2 Peel and finely chop the onion and garlic. Trim off the parsley stalks and pull the basil or oregano leaves from the stems; wash, blot dry with kitchen paper and chop finely. Finely chop the tomatoes or olives, discarding the stones.

3 Put the onion into a saucepan with the oil and fry over low heat, turning often, for 8–10 minutes or until soft and translucent but not brown; add the garlic and fry for 3–4 minutes more. Add the herbs and tomatoes or olives, season lightly with salt and more generously with pepper, and pour in the beans with their cooking water. Simmer for 20–25 minutes, adding more water if required. Finely grate the pecorino or Parmesan. Serve the soup sprinkled with plenty of cheese and accompanied by hot, crusty bread or Rusks (see page 15).

• CURRIED LENTIL AND •
MUSHROOM SOUP

This is a very pleasant, undemanding soup in which browned onions and button mushrooms accentuate the earthy taste of the lentils. The addition of coriander leaves is optional but a great improvement.

Serve with crusty bread or Rusks (see page 15). *For 3–4.*

• INGREDIENTS •

8 oz/250 g button mushrooms

2 medium/largish onions

3 cloves garlic

2 dried chillies

½ inch/1 cm piece
cinnamon stick

3 cloves

2 teaspoons coriander seeds

8 oz/250 g brown lentils

2 tablespoons olive oil

1½ level teaspoons Basic
Curry Powder (see page 62)

Salt

Small bunch coriander leaves
(enough for 1 tablespoon
when chopped)

Juice ½ small lemon

Wok or large saucepan with a lid

• METHOD •

1 Trim the mushroom stalks; wash the mushrooms and blot dry with kitchen paper; slice finely. Peel the onions and slice into half-rings. Peel and finely chop the garlic. Wash and dry the chillies and trim the stalk ends; empty or pick out the seeds and dice the flesh finely. Do not rub your eyes while chopping them and wash your hands directly afterwards (or wear polythene gloves). Crush the cinnamon, cloves and coriander seeds (start with the cinnamon, which is toughest). Rinse the lentils.

2 Put the onions into the wok or large saucepan and fry over low heat in the oil for 15 minutes or until pale brown; stir frequently, particularly towards the end. Add the garlic and fry for 3–4 minutes. Add the mushrooms and continue frying for 5–7 minutes or until soft. Add the chillies and turn in the oil. Stir in the spices and curry powder and cook for 1 minute. Add the lentils and 1¾ pints/1 litre water. Bring to the boil and boil briskly for 2 minutes, then lower the heat, cover and simmer for 35 minutes or until the lentils are very soft. Add ⅓ teaspoon salt and simmer for another 5–10 minutes. Trim the stems of the coriander, wash and blot dry with kitchen paper; chop the leaves. Add just before serving with lemon juice to taste.

·PASTA·

The enormous increase in the popularity of pasta means that you can now buy it fresh as well as dried in most supermarkets. The fresh is so much better that it seems pointless to compare them – but it is also two or three times as expensive. Moreover, despite a choice of thicknesses, shapes and flavours, it is (at the time of writing) virtually impossible to buy fresh wholemeal pasta: the only suppliers I have found are one or two London shops which do not normally sell it but will make it to order. You also cannot use fresh pasta for making cannelloni, as fresh cannelloni pipes will not keep their shape unless sold ready-filled.

Of the recipes in this chapter, the ones for which fresh pasta makes the most difference are Pasta with Peppers and Parsley Butter and Pasta with Courgettes and Basil Butter. Part of the attraction of both is their simplicity, which means that the quality of the pasta is particularly noticeable.

Fresh pasta should be stored in the refrigerator. If loose, it will stay moist for 24 hours; if packaged in an airtight container, for 48 hours.

I commented on the tastelessness of tomatoes in *The Student Cook Book*: one reason for it is that, in order to secure high yields, producers give their plants the most favourable conditions possible, whereas to achieve flavour unfavourable conditions – that is, poor soil and scarcity of water – are in fact necessary. Efforts to improve taste are being made, but at the moment most of the commercially grown tomatoes available need the addition of a substantial quantity of purée if they are to make an interesting sauce. It also helps to add a very small amount of sugar, which has a disproportionate effect in boosting sweetness. Other suggestions for improving flavour are to use ripe rather than hard fruit and to simmer the sauce for the full recommended time.

Whereas most of the dishes in the book will taste better if made with olive oil, it is especially desirable for pasta sauces. I have given the smallest practicable quantities of oil in all the recipes.

·To Cook Pasta·

·INGREDIENTS·

4–5 oz/125–150 g dried or 5–6 oz/150–190 g fresh pasta per person

1 teaspoon salt

Oil

·METHOD·

Pasta needs plenty of water. Bring a large saucepan three-quarters full of water to the boil over fairly high heat with the salt and a few drops of oil. Add the pasta. If using dried spaghetti, feed it in gradually so that it curls round the pan as it softens. Bring back to the boil and boil moderately fast either for as long as directed on the packet or, in the case of fresh pasta bought loose, for 1½–5 minutes: very narrow tagliarini will take 1½ minutes, tagliatelle 2–3 minutes and macaroni or largish shells 5 minutes. Some dried pasta is quick-cooking and needs only as little as 2 minutes, but ordinary dried may take 20 minutes. The pasta is ready ('*al dente*') when it can be cut with a blunt knife but still has 'bite'. Drain immediately, shake with a little oil or butter, to prevent it sticking together, and serve.

·Tomato and Herb Sauce·

You can make this sauce without herbs but it is more interesting with any of the following (listed in order of probable availability): dried oregano; fresh parsley, thyme, basil, coriander leaves, oregano. Alternatively it can be varied by adding spices and a red pepper, with or without chilli.

Use ripe, red tomatoes, which are not only sweeter than less ripe ones but easier to skin. Relatively unripe tomatoes will ripen in a day or two if left outside the refrigerator – but keep an eye on them to see that they do not become squashy or go mouldy.

Serve with spaghetti, tagliatelle or tagliolini and plenty of grated Parmesan or pecorino cheese (the dish includes no other high-protein ingredient). *For* 4.

• INGREDIENTS •

1½ *lb*/750 *g ripe tomatoes*

1 *medium onion*

3 *large cloves garlic*

1 *rounded teaspoon dried oregano or a handful fresh herbs as above (ideally, enough for 2 tablespoons when chopped, but less will do if you do not want to pick too much from small plants)*

1 *tablespoon olive oil*

1 *flat teaspoon soft brown sugar*

1½ *tablespoons tomato purée*

Salt

Pepper

• METHOD •

1 Peel and chop the tomatoes, throwing away the hard cores. Peel and finely chop the onion and garlic. If using fresh herbs, wash and leave in a sieve or colander to drain.

2 Fry the onion in the oil, turning frequently, for 8–10 minutes or until soft and translucent but not brown. Add the garlic and fry for 3–4 minutes more. Add the tomatoes and simmer for 7–10 minutes, pressing the flesh against the sides and bottom of the pan until smooth. Stir in the sugar, tomato purée and dried oregano if you are using it, season lightly with salt and more generously with pepper, and simmer for 25–30 minutes, stirring occasionally.

3 If using fresh herbs, trim the stalks off parsley or coriander and pull the leaves from the stems of other herbs; finely chop parsley, roughly chop coriander or oregano, or tear basil leaves into pieces. (Leave the tiny thyme leaves whole.) Stir into the sauce just before serving.

• SPICED TOMATO AND •
RED PEPPER SAUCE

The ingredients are as for Tomato and Herb Sauce (see page 35) but instead of herbs you will need 1 red pepper and 1 teaspoon coriander seeds.

• METHOD •

1 Peel and chop the tomatoes, throwing away the hard cores. Peel and finely chop the onion and garlic. Wash and quarter the red pepper, throwing away the core and removing any dark spots, the seeds (which are hot) and white inner membrane. Chop into sticks about ¾–1 inch/2–2.5 cm long and less than ¼ inch/5mm wide.

2 Fry the onion and red pepper in the oil over low heat, turning often, for 8–10 minutes as before; add the garlic, continue frying for 2 more minutes and add the coriander. Fry for 2–3 minutes. Add the tomatoes and simmer for 7–10 minutes, pressing out the lumps of flesh against the sides and bottom of the pan until smooth. Stir in the sugar and tomato purée, season lightly with salt and more generously with pepper, and simmer for 25–30 minutes, stirring occasionally.

• TOMATO AND CHILLI SAUCE •

The ingredients and method are as for Spiced Tomato and Red Pepper Sauce above, with the addition of 1 fresh or dried (preferably fresh) red chilli.

Wash the chilli after slicing the red pepper. Trim the stalk end and slit in half, discarding the seeds and (if fresh) the white inner pith. Cut into fine strips and dice as finely as possible. Do not rub your eyes while handling it and wash your hands immediately afterwards (or wear polythene gloves).

Add to the sauce with the coriander seeds and finish cooking as described above.

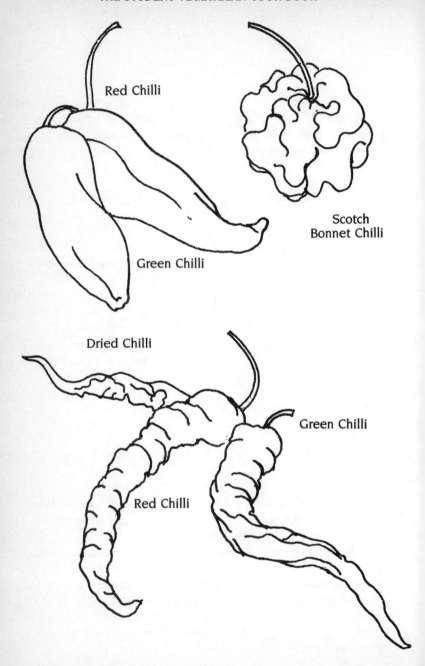

Red Chilli

Scotch
Bonnet Chilli

Green Chilli

Dried Chilli

Green Chilli

Red Chilli

• PESTO •

I have given this recipe before but am repeating it because it is a classic favourite and also because as well as serving it with pasta you can use it to add zest to other dishes.

It is very easy to make but calls for quite a lot of basil, and also pine nuts, which I am fully aware are expensive, although you do not need many.

You can use walnuts instead, but the result is quite different, since in this case the basil and cheese bring out the flavour of the nuts rather than the nuts enhancing the basil; nonetheless it is excellent in its own way. (Use only walnuts – other nuts do not work so well.)

I have given quantities for 2–3, because you may have only a small basil plant and not want to pick too many leaves. Take those from near the bottom of the stems rather than the top. *For 2–3.*

• INGREDIENTS •

2–3 fat sprigs parsley	*1 oz/25 g pine nuts*
About 16 basil leaves	*2 tablespoons olive oil*
1 oz/25 g Parmesan cheese	Salt
1 medium clove garlic	Pepper

• METHOD •

1 Trim off the parsley stems; pull the basil leaves from the stalks if necessary. Wash, blot dry with kitchen paper and roughly chop. Finely grate the cheese.

2 Peel and roughly chop the garlic and crush in a pestle and mortar. Add the chopped herbs, the nuts and 1 tablespoon of the oil (if you add all the oil at this stage, it will splatter). Pound to a thick paste.

3 Stir in the cheese, the remaining tablespoon of oil, a very little salt and slightly more pepper. The pesto is now ready to serve.

•WALNUT PESTO•

For this, use 1 oz/25 g walnut pieces instead of pine nuts and 3 not 2 tablespoons oil; otherwise, the recipe is as on page 39.

•SPINACH SAUCE•

The spinach takes 6–7 minutes to boil and can be cooked ahead of time (the day before if necessary); otherwise the sauce can be made in only about 5 minutes.

As its flavour depends on it, use real spinach (ideally pulled up by the roots), rather than Swiss chard or sea-kale beet, which have large, dark leaves and thick white stems and, although good in their own way, would be disappointing in this recipe.

Do not use skim-milk soft cheese as it may curdle when heated. Serve with spaghetti or tagliatelle and grated Parmesan. For 3–4.

• INGREDIENTS •

1 lb/500 g spinach	4 large cloves garlic
Salt	1 tablespoon olive oil
2 oz/50 g Parmesan cheese	½ oz/15 g butter
6 oz/190 g medium-fat soft cheese	

Large saucepan with a lid

• METHOD •

1 If the spinach was bought with roots, pull them off. Pick over, throwing away any weeds or damaged leaves, and wash, twice if necessary. Pack into the saucepan with 1 tablespoon water and ½ teaspoon salt, put on the lid and cook over medium heat for 5–6 minutes or until the spinach is submerged in juice and tender; stir once after about 4 minutes. Turn into a sieve or

colander set over a bowl and press out as much liquid as possible with the back of a spoon. Chop fairly finely. Add the cooking liquor to the water in which you boil the pasta. If you have cooked the spinach in advance, allow to cool, cover and store in the refrigerator until you need it; do the same with the cooking liquid if you have room (it is not, however, vital to the dish).

2 Grate the Parmesan. To ensure that it is not stiff, mash the soft cheese with a fork. Peel and finely chop the garlic. Warm the oil and butter over brisk heat in a frying-pan, add the garlic and shake for a moment or two until it has flavoured the oil and is beginning to change colour. Remove from the heat and stir in the spinach. Return to the heat very briefly, stirring continuously; remove, add and stir in the soft cheese, and very briefly heat again (if the cheese becomes too hot, it may turn stringy). Turn off the heat, stir in the Parmesan and serve immediately.

• INSTANT •
GORGONZOLA SAUCE

This really is instant. The first version is Mauro's, and also calls for sherry. If you have some, use it: it really does lift the sauce into something more than just liquid Gorgonzola. Without sherry, make it the second way. The fromage frais I use is fairly soft, but if yours is stiff add a little extra milk.

Serve with tagliatelle, tagliolini or other pasta. *For* 2.

• INGREDIENTS •

WITH SHERRY

4 oz/125 g Gorgonzola cheese	1 tablespoon medium or dry sherry
1 oz/25 g butter	A little pepper

WITH FROMAGE FRAIS

4 oz/125 g Gorgonzola cheese	1 tablespoon milk
2 oz/50 g plain fromage frais	A little nutmeg or pepper

• METHOD •

Beat the ingredients together with a fork and warm over low heat until most of the cheese is melted but a few solid lumps remain. Pour immediately over the cooked pasta.

• PASTA WITH PEPPERS• AND PARSLEY BUTTER

In this recipe the peppers do not form a sauce but are tossed straight into the pasta with the butter just before serving. It is very simple and quick: the only preparation needed is to wash and slice three peppers, chop an onion, garlic and parsley, and crush the parsley and an extra clove of garlic for the butter. The cooking takes 15 minutes.

The best time to make the sauce is in the autumn when peppers are cheapest. The peppers should be smooth and shiny: check to ensure that they have no soft patches (this applies particularly if they are pre-packaged).

Serve with tagliolini or narrow spaghetti and, for a well-balanced meal, plenty of grated Parmesan or pecorino cheese (apart from this, the dish contains no high-protein ingredient). *For 3.*

• INGREDIENTS •

1 red, 1 yellow and 1 green pepper	1½–2 oz/40–50 g butter
1 medium onion	Salt
4 medium to large and 1 small cloves garlic	Pepper
5–6 bushy sprigs parsley (enough for 2 tablespoons when chopped)	2 tablespoons olive oil

• METHOD •

1 Wash and quarter the peppers. Discard the core, seeds (which are hot) and white inner membrane and slice fairly

thinly, cutting out any dark spots on the red or yellow ones. Peel and finely chop the onion and four larger cloves of garlic; keep the onion and garlic separate. Trim the stalks of the parsley, wash, pat dry with kitchen paper and chop finely.

2 Peel, roughly chop and crush the small clove of garlic. Unless it is already soft, chop the butter into small pieces. Add it to the garlic with the parsley and a little salt and pepper (you will need very little salt if you are using salted butter) and pound till well mixed and the parsley is visible only as greenish flecks.

3 Put the peppers and onion into a frying-pan with the oil, season lightly with salt and pepper and fry over low heat, turning often, for 10–12 minutes or until the peppers are softening and the onion is just beginning to change colour. Add the garlic and continue frying, turning constantly, for 4–5 minutes or until the onion and garlic are golden and the peppers beginning to darken. Remove from the heat, add the parsley butter and toss into the hot pasta.

• MAURO'S CHICK PEA •
AND SPINACH SAUCE

Mauro is a seriously gastronomic Italian who runs a shop selling pasta, sauces and other Italian foods in Muswell Hill, North London. Most of his sauces contain meat or are for other reasons unsuitable for inclusion here, but the following is both simple and inexpensive, and the cheaper because it can be served without cheese, although you can sprinkle some over if you prefer (I think the slightly softer flavour of pecorino goes with it better than Parmesan).

As with Spinach Sauce, use real (fresh) spinach. Serve the sauce with tagliatelle or pasta shapes. *For 3–4.*

• INGREDIENTS •

*3 oz/90 g chick peas, soaked over-
night in cold water*

1 lb/500 g ripe tomatoes

Salt	1 *teaspoon cumin seeds*
1 *lb/500 g spinach*	2 *teaspoons coriander seeds*
5 *oz/150 g (1 large) onion*	1–1½ *tablespoons olive oil*
3–4 *cloves garlic*	Pepper
	3 *tablespoons tomato purée*

Large saucepan with a lid

• METHOD •

1 Drain the chick peas, rinse and discard any which are discoloured. Put them into the saucepan with a lid, add rather more water than will cover them (but no salt), bring to the boil, skim and boil briskly for 10 minutes. Cover and simmer for 1–1¼ hours; add extra water if necessary to keep them covered. Spinkle in a little salt and cook for 15–30 minutes more or until they break easily when prodded with a fork. Turn into a sieve or colander set over a bowl and reserve the cooking liquor.

2 Pick over the spinach and remove roots, weeds and damaged leaves. Wash, twice if necessary, and put into the large saucepan with ½ teaspoon salt and 1 tablespoon water. Put the lid on the pan and boil for 5–6 minutes or until the leaves are submerged and tender, stirring after about 4 minutes. Drain through a sieve or colander set over a bowl as for the peas: press out surplus water with the back of a spoon. Chop fairly finely. Use the cooking liquor to flavour the water in which you cook the pasta, to which, since the liquor is already seasoned, you will not need to add any more salt.

3 Peel and finely chop the onion and garlic. Peel and chop the tomatoes, cutting out the hard cores. Crush the cumin and

coriander. Fry the onion in the oil over low heat, turning frequently, for 8–10 minutes or until soft but not brown; add the garlic and fry for 2 minutes; stir in the cumin and coriander and fry for another 2–3 minutes. Add the tomatoes and simmer for 7–10 minutes, pressing out the lumps of flesh against the sides and bottom of the pan. Season very lightly with salt and a little more generously with pepper. Stir in the tomato purée and simmer for 20–25 minutes or until the sauce is thick. Add and stir in the chick peas.

4 Just before serving, stir in the spinach. If necessary, thin the sauce with ⅛–¼ pint/75–150 ml of the reserved chick pea liquor.

• PASTA WITH COURGETTES •
AND BASIL BUTTER

This is another very simple, quick-to-cook recipe – but if possible allow 30 minutes–1 hour for the courgettes to sweat before frying them. The actual cooking takes 15 minutes.

If there are any non-vegetarians present, they might like to sauté a few peeled prawns with their share: the result is simply too good not to be mentioned. Allow 1–1½ oz/25–40 g (shelled weight) prawns per head. Choose firm, glossy courgettes; small ones tend to have more flavour. Serve with largish shell pasta or tagliatelle (plain or flavoured; a mixture of spinach- and tomato-flavoured adds colour to the dish). As (prawns apart) no other high-protein ingredient is included serve with grated Parmesan cheese. For 4.

• INGREDIENTS •

1½ lb/750 g courgettes	7 cloves garlic
Salt, some of which should be finely ground	2 oz/50 g butter
	Pepper
Small bunch (at least 4 good-sized spears) basil	1½–2 tablespoons olive oil

• METHOD •

1 Wash the courgettes, pare off any brownish streaks or damaged patches of skin and trim the ends. Cut into slices ½ inch/1 cm thick. Sprinkle with fine salt and leave in a colander for 30 minutes–1 hour to sweat. Rinse under the cold tap and set on a plate lined with kitchen paper to dry.

2 Peel and roughly chop 1 clove of garlic. Wash the basil, blot dry with kitchen paper, pull off the leaves and tear them into pieces. Chop the butter into small dice. Put the chopped garlic into a mortar and crush. Add the butter and basil, season with a little salt (very little if the butter is salted) and slightly more pepper. Pound to a paste.

3 Peel and finely chop the rest of the garlic.

4 Make sure that the courgettes are dry (otherwise, the oil may spit when you put them into the pan). If necessary, wipe them with more kitchen paper. Place a large plate lined with fresh paper by the frying-pan. Put 1 tablespoon oil into the pan, warm it a little and add as many of the courgette slices as will fit over the bottom in one layer (you will probably have to fry them in two sessions). Season with very little salt but slightly more pepper and fry over medium to brisk heat for 2–3 minutes or until golden on each side. Set each slice when ready on the paper-lined plate to drain off surplus oil. Add more oil to the pan if necessary.

5 When all the slices are fried, pour just a little more oil into the pan, put in all the remaining garlic (unless some people are adding prawns) and allow it to fry until just starting to colour, shaking the pan so that it cooks evenly. Remove the pan from the stove and lower the heat. Put in all the courgette slices, set over lowish heat and turn gently for 1–2 minutes or until hot and crisp. Stir in the basil butter and serve as soon as it has melted.

Anyone who is adding prawns should reserve their share of uncooked garlic, fried courgette and butter, and fry the prawns in the pan with the garlic. Cooking is then finished as above.

· CANNELLONI WITH · SPINACH FILLING

If you have room in the refrigerator, you can prepare and assemble the whole dish in advance.

Do not use spinach substitutes (see page 27) in this recipe. If you are unable to buy real, fresh spinach, use frozen leaf spinach. *For 4–5.*

· INGREDIENTS ·

6 oz/190 g cannelloni pipes (you will probably have to buy an 8 oz/250 g packet)

FILLING

1½ lb/750 g spinach	*1 tablespoon oil*
Salt	*6 oz/190 g ricotta or other fresh-tasting medium-fat soft cheese*
3 oz/90 g Parmesan cheese	
3–4 cloves garlic	

TOMATO SAUCE

2 lb/1 kg ripe tomatoes	*Salt*
1 medium onion	*Pepper*
3–4 cloves garlic	*1 teaspoon soft brown sugar*
Small bunch parsley	*1½ generous tablespoons tomato purée*
1 tablespoon oil	

CHEESE SAUCE

¾ pint/450 ml milk	*¾ oz/20 g butter*
1 bayleaf	*¾ oz/20 g flour*
2 oz/50 g Gruyère cheese	*Salt*
2 oz/50 g Parmesan cheese	*Pepper*

Large saucepan with a lid

Ovenware dish about 12 inches/30 cm long, 10 inches/25 cm wide and 2½ inches/6 cm deep

• METHOD •

1 Make the filling. Pick over the spinach, removing any weeds or damaged leaves, and wash, twice if necessary. Pack into the saucepan with a lid and add ¾ teaspoon salt and 2 table-spoons water. Cover and set over medium heat for 4 minutes; stir and cook 2–3 minutes more or until the spinach is sub-merged in juice and tender. Drain and press out surplus liquid with the back of a spoon. Chop finely.

2 Grate the Parmesan. Peel and finely chop the garlic. Fry the garlic in the oil over medium heat for 20–30 seconds or until beginning to change colour. Remove from the heat and stir in the spinach. Allow to cool for a moment or two. Loosen the soft cheese with a fork if necessary and transfer to a bowl. Add and beat in the spinach and Parmesan. If made in advance, leave to cool, cover and store in the refrigerator.

3 Make the tomato sauce. Peel and chop the tomatoes, dis-carding the hard cores. Peel and finely chop the onion and garlic. Trim the parsley stems, wash the parsley, blot dry with kitchen paper and chop finely. Fry the onion in the oil over low heat, turning often, for 8–10 minutes or until soft but not brown. Add the garlic and fry for 3–4 minutes more. Add the tomatoes, season lightly with salt and more generously with pepper and continue frying for 7–10 minutes, pressing the tomato flesh against the bottom of the pan until it is liquified. Stir in the sugar and tomato purée. Simmer for 25 minutes or until thick, then stir in the chopped parsley. As with the filling, if made in advance, allow to cool, cover and put into the refrigerator.

4 To assemble the cannelloni, spread a third of the tomato sauce over the bottom of the ovenware dish. Stuff the pasta. This is fiddly and takes a little time. Use the point of a knife to push the spinach into the pipes: hold them over a plate in case the filling falls out at the other end. Put each filled pipe into the ovenware dish. When all the filling is used, pour the rest of the tomato sauce over the top.

5 Heat but do not boil the milk with the bayleaf, then remove from the heat and leave for 5–10 minutes to infuse. Pre-heat the oven to 400°F, 200°C, Gas Mark 6. Make the cheese sauce. Coarsely grate the Gruyère and the Parmesan. Melt the butter over low heat and add the flour. Stir until amalgamated, taking care not to let the mixture brown. Remove the bayleaf from the milk and pour the milk slowly into the butter and flour mixture, stirring continuously. Keep stirring until the sauce is thick. Allow to simmer for 4–5 minutes. Remove from the heat. Stir in a little salt and pepper, the Gruyère and most of the Parmesan (reserve some of the latter to sprinkle over the top).

6 Pour the cheese sauce over the cannelloni, taking care to cover the whole dish: if any of the pasta is left uncovered it will brown and become tough. Sprinkle the rest of the Parmesan over the top and bake in the oven for 15–20 minutes or until lightly browned.

·PASTRY·

There are several main types of pastry and any number of variations within the different types. The most generally useful, however, since it is used for tarts, quiches and some sorts of pie, is shortcrust, which is not supposed to rise but should be crisp and melting. Another kind, flaky pastry, is rolled several times with extra fat spread between the layers, which causes it to puff up; puff pastry is similar but with all the fat added between the layers, which makes it even puffier. A version of this is Greek filo pastry, which is paper-thin and layered with melted butter or oil rather than solid fat. The fact that an unsaturated oil can be used and its thinness, which means that there is altogether less of it, make it a healthier and less fattening alternative to ordinary pastry. However, to prepare it from scratch at home requires practice, and even in Greece it is customarily bought ready-made. I have included a recipe for it in Parties and Dinner-parties (see page 145); for the dishes in this chapter you need shortcrust or flaky pastry.

People think of even ordinary shortcrust pastry as difficult to make. This is chiefly for two reasons: that they find it hard to roll out, and that it becomes soggy when baked underneath moist fillings. The problem of rolling out varies according to the kind of flour you use. With white or a mixture of wholemeal and white, the dough tends to be sticky because the fat becomes warmer as it is worked. The solution is to keep it cold: it should be made with fat straight from the refrigerator and very cold water, and chilled for 20–30 minutes before rolling. With un-mixed wholemeal flour, on the other hand, the difficulty is that the dough crumbles. This is less easy to remedy than stickiness. Temperature is no help – in fact, chilling the dough before rolling makes it worse (though you should still make it with cold butter and water).

The answer lies in the composition of the dough: whereas shortcrust pastry is customarily made with a mixture of butter and other fat and a proportion of half as much fat as flour, if you want cohesive wholemeal dough you should use (I am afraid) only butter, and add a little oil. I have tried other possibilities, including using an egg, which works but gives a rather more solid, less 'short' result. I have also given a recipe for flaky pastry, which is mixed with cream and, provided that it is kept cool, infallibly rolls out very easily: it is ideal for pasties and the tops of pies, but not for tarts because it cannot successfully be 'blind-baked'.

'Blind-baking' (or partly baking) pastry is the answer to the problem of keeping it crisp under fillings. The usual method involves covering the pastry with aluminium foil so that it does not brown and preventing it from rising with rice or beans, which afterwards have to be thrown away (if it were not pre-baked, the filling would serve the same purpose). The pastry is then baked for a short time before the filling is added. The drawbacks to this are the waste of rice or beans and the fact that you have to heat the oven for longer than would otherwise be necessary. Obviously there is no way round prolonged use of the oven and I can only say that the result is worth it. In my experience, however, the rice or beans are not really essential, at any rate in the case of wholemeal pastry, which rises very little if at all. (For those who make pastry regularly, ceramic 'baking beans' are available.) Directions for blind-baking are given with the recipes.

Although I assume that most people will want to make wholemeal pastry, I have given a recipe for conventional short-crust using half wholemeal and half white flour, because for two items in particular (Pecan Pie and Polly's Chestnut Tarts with Hazelnut Pastry: see pages 141 and 153) I think the lighter crust is more suitable; you can also use it as an alternative for any of the recipes in this chapter.

Generally, pastry is crisper if made with plain rather than self-raising flour (the exception is cheese pastry: see page 144).

The dough can be made ahead of time – the previous day if you wish. Wrap it in foodwrap and store it in the refrigerator. You will need to allow a little time for it to soften before rolling it out: if it contains a mixture of flours, roll it while it is still fairly firm, as it would have been if it had been chilled; if it has been prepared entirely with wholemeal flour, leave it until it is as soft as when it was made.

You need slightly more liquid with wholemeal than with mixed flours.

•SHORTCRUST PASTRY WITH• WHOLEMEAL FLOUR

•INGREDIENTS•

4 oz/125 g butter straight from
the refrigerator

8 oz/250 g plain wholemeal flour,
plus extra for dusting

Salt

2 tablespoons cold water

½–1 tablespoon oil

**Rolling-pin (or clean milk or beer bottle)
Board or surface for rolling out
8½ inch/22 cm tart tin**

•METHOD•

1 Chop the butter into pieces about ½ inch/1 cm square. Mix the flour with a little salt: if the butter is unsalted, add a moderate pinch; if salted, very little.

2 Add the butter to the flour and rub it in with your fingertips until the mixture is like fine breadcrumbs. Make a well in the middle. Measure in the water and ½ tablespoon oil. Form into a ball, adding as much more oil as you need to take up all the flour and give a cohesive texture.

3 Generously dust the rolling-pin and board or rolling-out surface with flour. Set the tart tin conveniently near. Roll out the pastry until less than ¼ inch/5 mm thick. If it breaks, gather it up, sprinkle more flour over the rolling-pin and board and re-roll. Lift it carefully with a fish-slice or knife. Place it over the tin and press it gently into the edges. Trim, and patch any cracks with the trimmings (dampen undersides to stick).

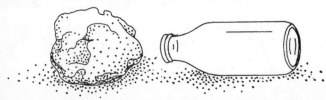

• SHORTCRUST PASTRY WITH •
WHOLEMEAL AND WHITE FLOUR

• INGREDIENTS •

2 oz/50 g butter straight from the refrigerator

2 oz/50 g hard vegetable shortening or margarine straight from the refrigerator

4 oz/125 g plain wholemeal flour

4 oz/125 g plain white flour, plus extra for dusting

Salt

2½ tablespoons cold water

Rolling-pin (or clean milk or beer bottle)
Board or surface for rolling out
8½ inch/22 cm tart tin

• METHOD •

1 Chop the fats into pieces about ½ inch/1 cm square. Blend the flours and a moderate pinch of salt.

2 Add the fat to the flour and rub it in with your fingertips until the mixture is like fine breadcrumbs. Make a well in the middle and add 2 tablespoons water. Form into a ball, adding more water gradually until all the flour is taken up. Do not add more than is necessary, since if the dough is too wet it will not only be sticky but the cooked pastry will be tough. As soon as it coheres (do not work it: the less it is handled the better), wrap it in foodwrap and chill for 20–30 minutes in the refrigerator.

3 Generously dust the rolling-pin and board or surface with white flour and set the tart tin near. Roll out the pastry firmly and quickly to a thickness of less than ¼ inch/5 mm. If it sticks to the board, gather it up, sprinkle more flour over the pin and board, and re-roll. Line the tin as described opposite.

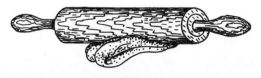

• FLAKY PASTRY •
WITH CREAM

Although the amount of flour used in this recipe is only half as much as for shortcrust pastry, it is sufficient to cover an 8½ inch/22 cm tart tin or dish.

This pastry is particularly good made with a mixture of granary and white flour.

Relatively accurate metric equivalents rather than convenient approximations are given here as precise proportions are important.

• INGREDIENTS •

2 oz/60 g granary flour and
2 oz/60 g plain white flour or
4 oz/125 g wholemeal flour,
plus extra for dusting

Salt

¼ pint/142 ml double cream

2 oz/50 g butter straight from
the refrigerator

Rolling-pin (or clean milk or beer bottle)
Board or surface for rolling out
8½ inch/22 cm tart tin or pie dish

• METHOD •

1 Blend the flour(s) and salt. Make a well in the middle and pour in the cream. Form into a ball, wrap in foodwrap and chill for 20–30 minutes in the refrigerator.

2 Cut the butter into 8 thin slices. Generously dust the rolling-pin and board or surface with flour. Roll the dough into a thick oblong. Sprinkle with flour, place 2 slices of butter on one half of it and fold into a square. Roll out and repeat 3 times until all the butter has been incorporated.

3 Set the tart tin or pie dish conveniently to hand. Flour the pin and board, then roll out the pastry as described for short-crust (see page 52), gathering it up and re-rolling if it sticks to the board or breaks. Line the tart tin.

• MUSHROOM AND •
WALNUT QUICHE

The flavours of all the ingredients in a quiche must be carefully balanced. In this one the yoghurt gives the eggs and cheese a sharpness which contrasts with the mushrooms and the richness of the nuts. To match the texture of the walnuts use small, firm button mushrooms. *For 4–5.*

• INGREDIENTS •

1 *quantity Shortcrust Pastry with Wholemeal Flour (see page 52) or Shortcrust Pastry with Wholemeal and White Flour (see page 53)*

8 *oz/250 g button mushrooms*

4 *cloves garlic*

2 *oz/50 g walnut pieces*

1 *heaped teaspoon coriander seeds*

4 *oz/125 g strong Cheddar cheese*

2 *oz/50 g Parmesan cheese*

1 *tablespoon oil*

Salt

Pepper

1 *teaspoon cornflour*

¼ *pint/150 ml (1 small carton) whole-milk yoghurt*

2 *eggs (size 2)*

2 *teaspoons mild French mustard (such as Grey Poupon)*

8½ inch/22 cm tart tin

• METHOD •

1 Pre-heat the oven to 400°F, 200°C, Gas Mark 6. Line the tart tin with the pastry. Cover all over, including the rim, with aluminium foil, pressing it closely to the edges of the tin. Bake in the oven for 10 minutes. Remove the foil and bake for another 5 minutes. Take the pastry case out of the oven.

2 Trim the stalks of the mushrooms, wash and blot dry with kitchen paper. Slice thinly. Peel and finely slice the garlic. Slightly crush or chop the walnuts. Crush the coriander. Grate the Cheddar and the Parmesan.

3 Fry the garlic in the oil over medium/lowish heat until the smell rises and it is just beginning to change colour. Add the coriander and fry for a few seconds, stirring constantly. Add the mushrooms, season moderately with salt and pepper, and fry for 7–8 minutes or until slightly browned, turning constantly. Add the nuts and turn for 1–2 minutes until crisp but not brown.
4 Mix the cornflour into the yoghurt. Beat in the eggs one by one and season moderately with salt and pepper. Add and stir in the cheeses and mustard. Stir in the nuts and mushrooms.
5 Pour the filling into the blind-baked pastry case and bake (still at 400°F, 200°C, Gas Mark 6) for 20–25 minutes or until slightly risen and just beginning to brown (because of the nuts, the quiche turns a particularly warm shade of golden-brown).

• ONION AND •
COURGETTE QUICHE

This quiche is designed to bring out the flavour of the onions. Its success depends on frying them to just the right shade of brown. Allow ½–1 hour for the courgettes to sweat. For 4–6.

• INGREDIENTS •

8–10 oz/250–310 (2 medium) courgettes

Salt, some of which should be finely ground

1 quantity Shortcrust Pastry with Wholemeal Flour (see page 52) or Shortcrust Pastry with Wholemeal and White Flour (see page 53)

1 lb/500 g (4 medium) onions

1 dried chilli

2 tablespoons oil

2 oz/50 g strong Cheddar cheese

2 oz/50 g Parmesan cheese

2 tablespoons milk

4 oz/125 g medium-fat soft cheese

2 eggs (size 2)

Pepper

8½ inch/22 cm tart tin

• METHOD •

1 Trim the ends of the courgettes; wash, peel off any damaged or discoloured patches of skin and chop into slices less than ¼ inch/5mm thick. Sprinkle with fine salt and put into a sieve or colander to sweat for 30 minutes–1 hour. Rinse under the cold tap and leave to drain.

2 Pre-heat the oven to 400°F, 200°C, Gas Mark 6. Line the tart tin with the pastry. Cover all over, including the rim, with aluminium foil, pressing it closely to the edges of the tin. Bake in the oven for 10 minutes. Remove the foil and bake for a further 5 minutes. Take the pastry case out of the oven.

3 Peel the onions and slice into rings about as thick as the courgette slices. Wash and dry the chilli and remove the stalk end. Slit lengthways, discard the seeds and dice as finely as possible; do not rub your eyes while chopping it and wash your hands directly afterwards (or wear polythene gloves).

4 If necessary, blot the courgettes dry with kitchen paper. Set a plate lined with fresh paper to hand. Fry the courgettes in the oil over medium heat for 2–3 minutes or until pale brown on each side. Place on the paper-lined plate to drain.

5 Allow the oil in the pan to cool a little. Then fry the onions over medium/low heat for 15–20 minutes or until lightly and evenly browned; turn constantly, particularly towards the end. Add the chilli and turn for 1–2 minutes. Remove from the heat.

6 Coarsely grate the Cheddar and Parmesan. Beat the milk into the soft cheese until smooth. Add and beat in the eggs one at a time. Season generously with salt and pepper and add the Cheddar and Parmesan, onions, chilli and courgettes. Pour into the half-cooked pastry case and bake (still at 400°F, 200°C, Gas Mark 6) for 20–25 minutes or until risen and golden.

• CURRIED EGG •
AND MUSHROOM PIE

This is supposed to be a shallow pie with pastry at the bottom as well as at the top. However, if you prefer, you can omit the pastry at the bottom and use Flaky Pastry with Cream for the top: in this case, to make the filling more liquid, add an extra tablespoon of bean water to the sauce.

You can make the pie in an ordinary tart dish, but it is much easier with a pie or other dish with a rim to hold the pastry.

Serve with baked potatoes, polenta, or vegetables.

If there is any pie left over, it is better eaten cold than hot, as the spices may become slightly bitter when reheated. For 5–6.

• INGREDIENTS •

2 oz/50 g red kidney beans, soaked overnight in cold water

Salt

8 oz/250 g large mushrooms

1 red pepper

2 medium onions

3 gloves garlic

1 teaspoon coriander seeds

1 dried chilli

4 eggs (size 2 or 3)

About 3 tablespoons oil

2 teaspoons Basic or Sambhar Curry Powder (see pages 62 and 63)

2½ teaspoons cornflour

½ lemon

3 tablespoons Greek or other mild, thick yoghurt

Shortcrust Pastry made with 12 oz/375 oz wholemeal flour, 6 oz/190 g butter, 3 tablespoons water and 1½ tablespoons oil (see page 52) or 1 quantity Flaky Pastry with Cream (see page 54)

**8½ inch/22 cm shallow pie or other ovenware dish with a rim
Saucepan with a lid**

• METHOD •

1 Drain the beans and rinse in cold water. Put into the saucepan, cover with water, bring to the boil, then skim (do not add salt). Boil fast for 10 minutes. Drain and return to the pan with fresh water (still without salt). Bring to the boil, reduce the heat, put the lid on the pan and simmer for 30 minutes; add a pinch of salt and continue simmering for 10 more minutes or until tender. Drain over a bowl to catch the cooking liquor, which is needed for the sauce.

2 Trim the mushroom stalks. Peel, rinse and dry the mushrooms and chop into ½ inch/1 cm cubes. Wash and quarter the pepper, removing the core, seeds and any dark spots, and dice the flesh. Peel and finely chop the onions and garlic. Crush the coriander seeds. Wash and dry the chilli and trim the stalk ends. Slit lengthways, shake or pick out all the seeds and dice the flesh as finely as possible. Do not rub your eyes while handling it and wash your hands directly afterwards.

3 Hard-boil the eggs: cover with water, bring to the boil and boil for 12 minutes. Put into cold water to cool. Shell and slice.

4 Pre-heat the oven to 400°F, 200°C, Gas Mark 6. If you are making the pie with a bottom crust, line the pie dish thinly with pastry (you will need slightly more than half). Cover all over with aluminium foil; press closely to the edges. Bake in the oven for 10 minutes. Remove the foil and bake for a further 5 minutes, then take it out of the oven. (If making the pie without a bottom crust, delay pre-heating the oven until after stage 5.)

5 Fry the onions and pepper in the oil over low heat, turning often, for 8–10 minutes or until soft but not brown. Add the garlic and fry for 3–4 minutes. Add the chilli and turn in the oil. Add the coriander and curry powder and fry for ½–1 minute, turning constantly. Add the mushrooms and fry for 5–7 minutes or until soft, still turning constantly. You may need to add a little more oil. Stir in 2 teaspoons of the cornflour. When amalgamated, add the beans and 8 fl oz/225 ml of their cooking liquor. Simmer for another 5–7 minutes or until the liquor has thickened. Remove from the heat. Wash the ½ lemon and grate in the zest. Mix the yoghurt with the remaining ½ teaspoon cornflour and stir into the sauce.

6 Put half the mixture into the partly baked bottom crust (or, if you are omitting it, into the pie dish). Arrange the slices of egg over it in a thick layer. Add the rest of the mixture. Roll out the pastry for the top. Brush the rim of the bottom crust (or pie dish) lightly with water to dampen it (if you have no pastry-brush, use damp kitchen paper) and cover the pie with the pastry lid. Trim the edges, cut pastry leaves or other shapes out of the trimmings, damp the undersides and use these to decorate the pie lid. Stamp the edges of the pie lid with a fork, make a steam hole in the middle and bake in the oven for 30 minutes or until lightly browned.

· RICE ·

There are two main types of rice, short-grain, which releases starch during cooking and is used for puddings and risottos, and long-grain, which is suitable for pilaf and to accompany stir-fried dishes and curries. Various sorts within each type are grown: for risotto, I recommend *arborio*, which has a firm but slightly glutinous texture; for pilafs, stir-fries and curries the most widely available are American long-grain and Indian Patna and Basmati. Basmati, which has a particularly elongated grain, is about a third more expensive than American rice or Patna but worth it on occasion for its distinctive, nutty flavour. All the long-grain sorts are available in brown, which is preferable in terms of both nutrition and flavour for all purposes except risotto, where a soft, creamy texture is desirable.

In this chapter I have included recipes not only for a pilaf and a risotto, but also for spice mixtures and a curry (there are more curries elsewhere in the book). Making your own curry powder does not take long and in fact is rather fun; it produces a mixture with far more character and flavour than the average commercial version.

I owe my introduction to Eastern culinary ideas to two writers in particular: Yan-kit So, whose Wok Cookbook first inspired me to try stir-frying and on whose instructions my own technique is based (see next chapter); and Jill Norman, author of The Complete Book of Spices, which anyone who enjoys using spices should read. I have given three of her recipes in this book almost without alteration, not least because the testing team, having tried several others, declared that they liked hers best.

· TO COOK RICE ·

By far the simplest and healthiest way of cooking rice is to simmer it in just as much water as it will absorb. This cuts out draining and reheating and means that none of its nutrients are poured away with the cooking water. As rice varies slightly in absorbency, a little extra liquid may be needed towards the end of cooking or a slight surplus evaporated, so that the result is light, dry and separate-grained. *For 4.*

• INGREDIENTS •

1 *lb*/500 *g long-grain brown rice* (*this is generous: you may prefer to cook less, in which case reduce the amount of water proportionately*)

1½ *pints*/900 *ml water*

Few drops oil

Salt

Saucepan with a lid

• METHOD •

Rinse the rice under the cold tap to remove any surplus starch on the surface of the grains. Put the rice, water and oil into the saucepan with a generous pinch of salt and bring to the boil. Reduce the heat, cover and simmer for 20 minutes. Check to ensure that there is still a little liquid in the pan and add more water if necessary. Simmer for 10 more minutes or until the rice is tender: test by breaking a grain between the thumb and forefinger or by tasting. Basmati rice should take just 30 minutes, Patna and American long-grain 30–35 minutes. If there is any water left in the saucepan, raise the heat to moderate until it has evaporated. If kept covered after removal from the heat, the rice will stay hot for 10–15 minutes.

•JILL NORMAN'S• CURRY POWDERS

There are two points about making curry powder which should be emphasised. The first is that the spices are toasted, which creates a potent smell, so if you have an extractor fan in your kitchen it is advisable to use it; otherwise open the window or better still an outside door before you start. The second is that the powders are strong especially just after they are made: broadly speaking, 2 teaspoons are all you need for 4.

I am giving a choice of two powders: I like the first, which is less strong, but the testing team preferred the second. As Jill Norman stresses, you can alter the proportions of the ingredients to suit yourself, or add others. Basic Curry Powder, for instance, can be made with half the recommended quantity of chillies and turmeric but with the addition of a ¾ inch/2 cm length of cinnamon stick and 4–5 cloves.

If stored in an airtight container (a plastic freezing-carton with a fitted lid is ideal), the powders will stay fresh for a few months, but will become milder the longer you keep them.

• BASIC CURRY POWDER •

Jill's recipe calls for fresh curry leaves, which are difficult to find. As dried ones, although easier to buy, have little flavour, I have omitted curry leaves completely: the powder is still excellent.

• INGREDIENTS •

6 dried chillies	½ teaspoon mustard seeds
2 teaspoons cumin seeds	½ teaspoon ground ginger
1 oz/25 g coriander seeds	1 teaspoon fenugreek seeds
1 teaspoon black peppercorns	1 tablespoon ground turmeric

Thick saucepan

• METHOD •

1 Wash and thoroughly dry the chillies. Trim the stalk ends, shake or pick out the seeds and chop the flesh as finely as possible. Put into a mortar. Do not rub your eyes while handling them and wash your hands directly afterwards (or wear polythene gloves).
2 Put the cumin seeds into the thick saucepan and toast over moderate heat for 1–2 minutes or until they begin to change colour; shake the saucepan constantly to prevent burning. As

soon as they start darkening, tip them into the mortar. (It is important to transfer them promptly because the heat of the saucepan will cause them to continue cooking.)

3 Toast the other seeds, shaking the pan constantly, for 1–3 minutes (the time depends partly on the previous heat of the pan) until all but the peppercorns start to darken. Tip into the mortar. Add the ginger and turmeric and pound to a fine powder (the finer, the better; the spices are less likely to burn when you fry them than if they are coarsely crushed). This does not take long, for the toasted spices crush easily. Check that the mixture has cooled and transfer to an airtight container.

• SAMBHAR POWDER •

Asafoetida can be bought at good health-food shops. The original recipe calls for white gram beans: I have substituted split peas. Their function is to give the mixture body and to thicken the curry sauce very slightly.

• INGREDIENTS •

10 *dried chillies*	½ oz/15 g *fenugreek seeds*
¾ oz/20 g *cumin seeds*	¼ *teaspoon asafoetida*
1 oz/25 g *coriander seeds*	1 *tablespoon ground turmeric*
1 *teaspoon mustard seeds*	1 *tablespoon oil*
½ oz/15 g *black peppercorns*	2 oz/50 g *yellow split peas*

Thick saucepan

• METHOD •

1 Wash, dry, de-seed and dice the chillies as described for Basic Curry Powder. Put into a mortar.

2 Toast the cumin seeds in the thick saucepan, shaking constantly, for 1–2 minutes or until they begin to darken, then immediately tip into the mortar. Toast the other seeds and add these to the mortar also.

3 Toast the asafoetida and turmeric until they start to darken: this takes only a few seconds. Add to the other ingredients and crush everything to a fine powder. Turn into a bowl.

4 Heat the oil over medium heat in the saucepan and fry the peas in the oil until deep orange. Transfer to the mortar, leaving behind any surplus oil. Crush as thoroughly as possible (they are more difficult to pulverise than the spices). Stir into the spice mixture. Allow to cool and store in an airtight container.

• JILL NORMAN'S • GARAM MASALA

This is an aromatic mixture which can be used as an additional flavouring to curries or other dishes. It will have a more obvious effect if added about half-way through or at the end of cooking rather than at the beginning. I have slightly modified the original recipe.

• INGREDIENTS •

1 *stick cinnamon*	2 *teaspoons green cardamom pods*
2 *bayleaves*	2 *teaspoons cloves*
3 *teaspoons cumin seeds*	1 *teaspoon black peppercorns*
1 *tablespoon coriander seeds*	⅔ *nutmeg*

Thick saucepan

• METHOD •

1 Break up and crush the cinnamon using a pestle and mortar. Chop or crumble the bayleaves as finely as possible and add to the mortar.

2 Toast the cumin seeds in the thick saucepan over medium heat, shaking constantly, for 1–2 minutes or until they start to darken. Tip straight away into the mortar.

3 Toast the coriander, cardamom, cloves and peppercorns for 1–3 minutes or until they start to change colour. Put into the mortar. Finely grate in the nutmeg. Pound the mixture to a fine powder, check it has cooled and store in an airtight container.

•VEGETABLE CURRY•
WITH ALMONDS

This is a quickly cooked, dry curry, which is especially suitable for vegetables. It is light and aromatic rather than strong: the aim is to achieve a balance of flavours. *For* 3.

• INGREDIENTS •

2½ oz/75 g whole almonds

1 red pepper

8 oz/250 g button mushrooms

2 medium onions

3 cloves garlic

2 teaspoons coriander seeds

1 teaspoon poppy seeds

1 lemon

2 dried chillies

8 oz/250 g broccoli

Salt

1 scant teaspoon Jill Norman's Garam Masala (see page 64)

2 tablespoons oil

1½ teaspoons Basic or Sambhar Curry Powder (see pages 62 and 63)

Thick saucepan
Saucepan with a lid
Wok or large saucepan with a lid

• METHOD •

1 Toast the almonds: put into the thick saucepan and shake over medium heat for 2 minutes or until just starting to change colour. Immediately tip on to a plate (if left in the hot saucepan, they will continue to cook). A better result is achieved by baking but it hardly seems worthwhile to turn on the oven specially: if you prefer, however, bake them on a baking-sheet lined with aluminium foil at 400°F, 200°C, Gas Mark 6, for 5–6 minutes.

2 Wash, dry and quarter the pepper, discarding the core and seeds. Cut out the white inner membrane and any dark spots and dice the flesh. Trim the mushroom stalks. Wash the mushrooms, blot dry with kitchen paper and slice. Peel the onions and slice into fine rings. Peel and finely chop the garlic. Crush the seeds.

3 Wash the lemon. Grate the zest and squeeze half of it; cut the rest into wedges. Wash and dry the chillies. Remove the stalk end, slit, and pick out the seeds; dice as finely as possible. Do not rub your eyes while handling them and wash your hands directly afterwards.

4 Wash the broccoli and chop into florets 1 inch/2.5. cm long, ½ inch/1.5 cm wide at the flower end, and not more than ¼ inch/5 mm wide at the stalk end. Put into the saucepan (not the wok) with a lid, just cover with water, bring to the boil and boil for 5–6 minutes or until tender but still crisp. Drain and return to the saucepan. Sprinkle with the garam masala, toss thoroughly and cover.

5 Heat the oil in the wok or large saucepan and fry the pepper and onions with the curry powder and chilli over medium heat, turning frequently, for 5–7 minutes or until soft. Add the garlic and fry for 2–3 minutes. Add the mushrooms and fry for 5–7 minutes or until soft, turning continuously. Add the coriander and poppy seeds and fry for 1–2 minutes. Add the broccoli, toss and fry for 1 minute; stir in the almonds, sprinkle with the lemon zest, cover and leave for 2–3 minutes. Add the lemon juice and serve on a bed of rice with the wedges of lemon and a generous bowl of yoghurt.

• MUSHROOM RISOTTO •

I was tempted to call this 'Rosy Risotto' because of its rosy, sunset colour. It is very much a recipe with a holiday feel.

It is much better prepared with white than with brown rice. Brown mutes the colour and flavour, whereas the sticky, nutty texture of white Italian *arborio* rice suits its character. As white rice also cooks more quickly than brown, using it means that the risotto can be on the table in just over an hour flat.

If possible, choose large or a mixture of large and button mushrooms. Besides being quicker to prepare, large ones tend to have more flavour than buttons; a few buttons mixed with them, however, will add interest to the texture of the dish.

Serve with Parmesan cheese for sprinkling. *For 3–4.*

• INGREDIENTS •

1 lb/500 g large mushrooms or about 10 oz/310 g large ones and 6 oz/190 g buttons

1 large red pepper

1 lb/500 g ripe tomatoes

2 medium onions

4 cloves garlic

2 teaspoons coriander seeds

1 fresh or dried red chilli

2 tablespoons olive oil

Salt

Pepper

2 tablespoons tomato purée

12 oz/375 g white arborio rice

2 oz/50 g pine nuts (optional)

At least 3 oz/90 g Parmesan cheese to serve

Large saucepan with a lid
Small baking-sheet

• METHOD •

1 Trim the mushroom stalks; peel, rinse and dry large mushrooms and wash and dry button ones. Leave very small buttons whole; chop others into slices about ¼ inch/5 mm thick.

2 Wash, dry and quarter the red pepper, discarding the core and seeds; remove the white inner membrane and any dark spots and cut the flesh into strips about as thick as the mushrooms and 1¼ inches/3 cm long. Peel and chop the tomatoes, cutting out the cores. Peel and finely chop the onions and garlic. Crush the coriander. Wash and dry the chilli, and chop off the stalk end; slit lengthways, pick out the seeds and dice the flesh as finely as possible. Do not rub your eyes while handling it, and wash your hands directly afterwards.

3 Fry the onions and pepper in 2 tablespoons oil, turning frequently, for 8–10 minutes or until the onion is soft and translucent but not brown. Add the garlic and chilli and fry for 2 minutes. Add the coriander and fry for 2–3 minutes. Add the mushrooms, season lightly with salt and moderately with pepper, and continue frying, turning very often, for 5–7 minutes or until soft; you may find that you need a little more oil. Add the tomatoes, season very lightly, and simmer for a further 7–10 minutes, pressing out the lumps of flesh against the sides and bottom of the pan until liquified. Stir in the tomato purée. Add 1¼ pints/750 ml water and the rice. Bring to the boil, turn down the heat, cover and simmer for 18–20 minutes or until the rice is swollen and tender but still has bite: test by breaking a grain between the thumb and forefinger. Nearly all the liquid will have been absorbed, but there should be just enough left to moisten the risotto and act as a sauce.

4 If you are using pine nuts, pre-heat the oven to 350°F, 180°C, Gas Mark 4, after adding the rice to the vegetables (this is to toast the nuts, which is not vital but will crispen them and bring out their flavour). When the rice has cooked for 10 minutes, spread the nuts on a baking-sheet and roast in the oven for 6–7 minutes, or until lightly browned, turning to ensure even cooking after about 4 minutes. Grate the Parmesan. Stir the pine nuts into the risotto as soon as the rice is cooked and serve accompanied by the grated Parmesan sprinkled over the top according to taste.

•PEPPER AND NUT PILAF•

In terms of flavour this really does not need any addition but, as pilaf is drier than risotto, you may prefer to stir in a few raisins and serve it with yoghurt as suggested below.

For a really special dish, make the pilaf with saffron and Basmati rice, the nutty taste and texture of which accentuate the nuts in the pilaf. Choose firm, glossy peppers, button rather than open mushrooms and smaller courgettes (which tend to have more flavour). Take care to use plain roasted peanuts, not salted ones.

• INGREDIENTS •

8 oz/250 g (2 smallish) courgettes

Salt, some of which should be finely ground

2 sticks celery

1 lb/500 g fresh unshelled or 8 oz/250 g frozen peas

1 medium onion

3 cloves garlic

1 red and 1 yellow pepper

4 oz/125 g button mushrooms

1½ generous teaspoons coriander seeds

12 oz/375 g brown Patna, American long-grain or Basmati rice

Pinch saffron threads (optional)

2 tablespoons oil

Pepper

2 oz/50 g pine nuts

2 oz/50 g hazelnuts

2 oz/50 g unsalted roasted peanuts

OPTIONAL ACCOMPANIMENT

2 oz/50 g raisins

7 oz/225 g Greek or Greek-style yoghurt

Large saucepan with a lid

• METHOD •

1 Wash the courgettes, trim the ends and pare off any brownish streaks or damaged pieces of skin. Cut into slices about ¼ inch/5 mm thick, sprinkle with fine salt and leave to sweat in a colander for 30 minutes–1 hour. Rinse under the cold tap and set to dry on a plate lined with kitchen paper.

2 Trim the leaf and root ends of the celery, pare off any brown streaks, wash and cut into slices about ¼ inch/5 mm wide. Put into a saucepan with ½ pint/300 ml water and a generous pinch of salt, bring to the boil and boil gently for 7–10 minutes or until just tender. Drain over a bowl and set aside; keep the cooking liquor.

3 Shell the peas if necessary. Put into a saucepan with ¾ pint/450 ml water. Bring to the boil and boil gently for 5–8 minutes or until tender if fresh, or for 3 minutes if frozen. Drain over the bowl containing the celery liquor and set aside.

4 Peel and finely chop the onion and garlic, keeping each separate. Wash and quarter the peppers; throw away the cores and seeds (which are hot) and trim off the white inner membrane and any dark spots. Cut the flesh into strips of about the same thickness as the slices of celery and courgette. Trim the mushroom stalks; wash the mushrooms and dry on kitchen paper, and slice each into 3 or 4 pieces. Crush the coriander.

5 Rinse the rice. Measure the celery-and-pea liquor and add water if necessary to make it up to 1⅛ pints/675 ml. Pour into the saucepan with a lid and add the saffron if you are using it, a drop of oil and the rice. Bring to the boil, lower the heat to a simmer, put on the lid and cook for 20 minutes; look at the rice and, if it seems dry, add about another 3 fl oz/75 ml water. Replace the lid and continue to simmer for 5–10 minutes or until the rice is just tender: test by breaking a grain between the thumb and forefinger. Remove from the heat and leave the lid on the pan until you are ready to add the other ingredients.

6 Check that the the courgettes are dry: if necessary, blot them with more kitchen paper. Put a plate lined with fresh kitchen paper alongside the cooker. Warm the oil in a frying-pan over medium to brisk heat and add the courgette slices in a single layer. Season very lightly with salt and more moderately with pepper and fry for 2–3 minutes, or until golden, on each side. Place the slices when cooked on the paper-lined plate to drain off surplus oil. Remove the pan from the heat for a moment to cool the remaining oil, lower the heat and put in the onion and peppers. Cook slowly, turning often, for 8–10 minutes or until the onion is soft and translucent. Add the garlic and fry for about 2 minutes; add the coriander and cook for 2–3 minutes more. Add the mushrooms, season moderately and continue frying for another 7–10 minutes, turning very frequently, until the peppers are soft. Add the nuts and turn continuously for about 2 minutes. If you are going to serve the pilaf with yoghurt, add the raisins now and turn for another minute or so. Stir in the courgettes, celery and peas. Empty the contents of the frying-pan into the cooked rice and mix thoroughly. Serve with the yoghurt in a separate bowl. If there is any pilaf left over (or if you made it in advance), cool, cover and store in the refrigerator. Reheat in a covered casserole in the oven for 20–25 minutes at 400°F, 200°C, Gas Mark 6.

·STIR-FRIED· VEGETABLES

Stir-frying is a wonderfully quick way of turning ingredients which might otherwise be bland into a dish with zest and interest. This is achieved partly with flavourings, notably ginger and soy sauce, and also by very swift cooking, which especially suits vegetables because they retain not only their original crispness but a relatively high proportion of nutrients too.

The basic technique is to chop the ingredients very small and fry them for a matter of minutes over high heat, stirring continuously to ensure even cooking. Non-liquid flavourings are put into the pan first so that their flavour is imparted to the oil; items are then added in order of cooking time – that is, those needing longest are added first – and soy sauce stirred in at the very end. Rice can be served separately so that the ingredients act as a sauce, or it may be mixed with them as part of the dish.

Most vegetables can be cooked in this way. Those which cannot include peas and podded beans, sea-kale beet (as opposed to spinach) and, rather obviously, tomatoes. Most also take 2–3 minutes to fry but some, such as aubergines, peppers, cabbage, cauliflower and broccoli, take longer. The last three are more successful if boiled briefly first (cabbage fried long enough to be tender tends to burn). A selection of 3 or 4 vegetables will make an attractively varied dish: choice can be governed by prices and preference, but bear in mind that (as with salads) texture and colour play a part as well as flavour; to make a balanced meal, you also need to add a high-protein ingredient such as bean-sprouts, nuts, seeds or egg. Except those which need boiling and aubergines and courgettes, which need salting, the vegetables should be chopped directly before frying to minimise loss of vitamin C.

Always use fresh root ginger. If this is not available, omit ginger altogether.

The quantities are for 2–3 because this amount can comfortably be stir-fried in an average-sized wok or largish saucepan.

71

• STIR-FRIED TOFU WITH •
MUSHROOMS AND SPINACH

Plain tofu (soya bean curd) has very little taste of its own but readily absorbs other flavours: hence when smoked it acquires a particularly distinctive smokiness which is delicious with cheese and certain vegetables. In this recipe its character is emphasised by the spinach and pine nuts; the mushrooms match it in texture and the celery adds bite. It is essential to use real, fresh spinach. *For 2–3.*

• INGREDIENTS •

4 oz/125 g spinach

8 oz/250 g brown Patna, American long-grain or Basmati rice

Salt

About 3 tablespoons oil

4 oz/125 g button mushrooms

2 large sticks celery

2 large sticks celery

4 oz/125 g smoked tofu

½ inch/1 cm piece fresh root ginger

3 cloves garlic

2 tablespoons soy sauce (preferably light)

1 oz/25 g pine nuts

Saucepan with a lid
Wok or large saucepan

• METHOD •

1 Pick over the spinach, removing all weeds and damaged leaves; pull off the roots and break off and discard any long stems. Wash, twice if necessary, and drain.

2 Rinse the rice. Put into the saucepan with a lid and add ¾ pint/450 ml water, a good pinch of salt and a few drops of oil. Bring to the boil, lower the heat and simmer, covered, for 30 minutes for Basmati or 30–35 minutes for Patna or American long-grain rice; test to see if it is tender by breaking a grain between the thumb and forefinger. If necessary, simmer a few more minutes, adding just a little extra water if it is very dry. Keep covered until you are ready to serve.

3 Trim the stalks of the mushrooms; wash them and leave on a plate lined with kitchen paper to dry. Cut the leaves off the celery sticks and trim the root ends, pare off any brown streaks, wash and cut into slices about ¼ inch/5 mm thick. Leave to dry on a second plate lined with kitchen paper. Drain the tofu if necessary and cut into sticks ¼ inch/5 mm across and ½ inch/ 1 cm long; put on another plate. Peel and finely slice the garlic. Peel, wipe if necessary and finely slice the ginger, discarding any bits which are tough or stringy.

4 Cut the spinach into strips about ½ inch/1 cm across; if still damp, dry by laying on another paper-lined plate and blotting. Blot the mushrooms if necessary (it is essential that all the ingredients to be fried are dry or the oil will spit) and cut into slices ¼ inch/5 mm thick. Blot the celery if still damp.

5 Set all the prepared ingredients plus the soy sauce to hand. Put 3 tablespoons oil into the wok or large saucepan and warm for a moment or two over high heat. Add the garlic and ginger and allow to fry (do not stir yet) until the smell of the ginger in particular becomes noticeable and they are just beginning to colour. This takes only a few seconds. Add the celery and tofu and fry, stirring continuously, for 1 minute or until the celery looks slightly less opaque. Add the mushrooms and continue to stir-fry for about 30 seconds. Add the spinach and stir-fry for 1 minute or until the mushrooms are soft and the spinach reduced but not ragged. Add the nuts and stir; stir in the soy sauce. Remove from the heat and serve on top of the rice.

• STIR-FRIED BROCCOLI AND • RED PEPPER WITH PEAS

With the dark green broccoli, bright green peas and pale green celery, this is very, very green – except for the pepper, which against this background looks almost fluorescent. As peas cannot be stir-fried (they simply split and disintegrate), they are cooked separately and added at the end. *For 2–3.*

• INGREDIENTS •

8 oz/250 g broccoli	4 oz/125 g (3–4 sticks) celery
Salt	1 red pepper
1 lb/500 g fresh unshelled or 8 oz/250 g frozen peas	3 cloves garlic
8 oz/250 g brown Patna or American long-grain rice	⅔ inch/1.5 cm piece fresh root ginger
About 3 tablespoons oil	3 teaspoons light (preferable) or 2 teaspoons dark soy sauce

Small saucepan
Saucepan with a lid
Wok or large saucepan

• METHOD •

1 Wash the broccoli and cut into florets about 1 inch/2.5 cm long and ½–⅔ inch/1–1.5 cm across at the flower end. Bring about ⅔ pint/400 ml slightly salted water to the boil in the small saucepan, put in the broccoli, bring back to the boil and boil briskly for 2 minutes. Turn into a sieve set over a bowl to catch the cooking water, rinse under the cold tap and leave on a plate lined with kitchen paper to dry. (You will need the sieve to drain the peas.)

2 Shell the peas if necessary. Just cover with slightly salted, cold water, bring to the boil and boil gently for 5–8 minutes or until tender if fresh, or for 3 minutes if frozen. Drain over the bowl of broccoli water and set aside.

3 Rinse the rice and put into the saucepan with a lid. Add ¾ pint/450 ml of the pea-and-broccoli liquor, a few grains of salt and two or three drops of oil. Bring to the boil, reduce the heat to a simmer, cover and cook for 30–35 minutes or until tender: test by breaking a grain between the thumb and forefinger. If necessary, add just a little more water. Keep covered until you are ready to serve.

4 Trim the leaf and root ends of the celery, pare off any brown streaks, wash and cut into slices ¼ inch/5 mm thick. Spread on a plate lined with kitchen paper to dry. Wash and quarter the pepper, removing the seeds (which are hot), any dark spots and the white inner membrane; cut the flesh into strips about the same width as the celery and ¾ inch/2 cm long. Set to dry on a second paper-lined plate. Peel and finely slice the garlic. Peel, wipe if necessary and finely slice the ginger, discarding any tough or fibrous pieces.

5 Check that all the vegetables are dry; blot with more kitchen paper if necessary. Place all the prepared vegetables and the soy sauce within reach. Put 3 tablespoons oil into the wok or large saucepan and warm for a moment or two over high heat. Add the garlic and ginger and allow to fry for a few seconds (do not stir yet) until just starting to change colour. Add the pepper and stir-fry for 1½ minutes. Add the celery and stir-fry for a few seconds; add the broccoli and stir-fry for 2–3 minutes or until the celery is tender but still crisp and the broccoli soft but the florets not disintegrating. Stir in the peas. Add the soy, stir and remove from the heat. Serve on top of the rice.

• STIR-FRIED BEANS AND • PEPPERS WITH EGGS

If described as an omelette chopped up and reheated, the eggs in this recipe would not sound particularly attractive – whereas in my view this is one of the best possible ways of cooking them. Both here and in the following recipe for Stir-fried Beans and Peppers with Fried Rice and Eggs (which is much less omelette-like) their flavour comes through remarkably clearly despite the rice and other ingredients, which are designed to complement it and add texture.

You need only a quarter of a cabbage for this recipe, and to keep the remainder as fresh as possible for another meal it is best to slice as much as you need from one side, peeling off the outermost leaves if they are coarse or stringy. Wrap the part which will not be used in foodwrap and store in the refrigerator. For 2–3.

• INGREDIENTS •

4 oz/125 g (about ¼ small) cabbage

Salt

8 oz/250 g brown Patna, American long-grain or Basmati rice

About 5 tablespoons oil

4 oz/125 g button mushrooms

4 oz/125 g Kenya or other stringless green beans

1 red or yellow pepper or (preferably) ½ of each

2–3 spring onions

½ inch/1 cm piece fresh root ginger

3 eggs (any size)

Pepper

3 teaspoons soy sauce (preferably light)

Saucepan with a lid
Wok or large saucepan

• METHOD •

1 Remove any tough stalks from the cabbage leaves and cut the leaves into ½ inch/1 cm squares; wash. Bring 1 pint/600 ml slightly salted water to the boil, put in the cabbage, return to the boil and boil for 2 minutes. Drain in a sieve set over a bowl to catch the cooking water. Rinse and leave to dry.

2 Rinse the rice and put into the saucepan with a lid. Add ¾ pint/450 ml of the cabbage water, a few drops of oil and a very little salt. Bring to the boil, lower the heat to a simmer, cover and simmer for 30 minutes for Basmati, 30–35 for Patna or American long-grain rice: test to see if it is tender by breaking a grain between the thumb and forefinger. If necessary, simmer a few more minutes, adding a little extra water if it is dry. Keep covered until you are ready to serve.

3 Trim the mushroom stalks and wash the mushrooms. Top and tail the beans, cut into sticks about 1 inch/2.5 cm long and wash. Leave both to dry on plates lined with kitchen paper. Wash, dry and quarter the pepper, discarding the core; remove any dark spots and seeds (which are hot), trim off the white inner membrance and cut the flesh into strips about ¼ inch/ 5 mm wide and ¾ inch/2 cm long. Leave on another plate. Cut off the leaves and roots of the onions, peel off the outer layer and thickly slice the white part. Peel, wipe and thinly slice the ginger, throwing away any tough or fibrous pieces.

4 Check that the mushrooms are dry and blot with kitchen paper if necessary. Cut into slices about ¼ inch/5 mm thick. Blot the beans and cabbage if necessary. Beat the eggs with a fork and season fairly generously with salt and pepper.

5 Set a large plate to hand. Put 2 tablespoons oil into the wok or large saucepan. Warm over medium heat for a moment or two, tilting the wok (if using one) so that it coats the sides (this is to prevent the egg from sticking: it is not necessary if the wok is non-stick). Pour in the egg and tip the pan so that it spreads over the sides or bottom. Use a spoon or fish-slice to turn it towards the middle as it sets, continuing to tip the pan so that the part which is still runny slides to the bottom. Repeat until all the egg is just (but only just) set. Remove from the heat, lift on to a plate and chop into pieces about ⅓ inch/8 mm square. Wash or wipe the wok or saucepan.

6 Place all the prepared vegetables and the soy sauce within reach. Put 3 tablespoons oil into the wok or pan and warm for a moment or two over high heat. Add the ginger and allow to fry for a few seconds. Add the onions and fry for another few seconds. Add the pepper and fry, stirring continuously, for 1½–2 minutes or until it begins to look slightly seared. Add the beans and stir-fry for 1 minute. Add the mushrooms and cabbage and stir-fry for 1–2 minutes or until the mushrooms are soft and the cabbage tender but not mushy. Stir in the egg. Add and stir in the soy sauce. Remove from the heat and serve on top of the rice.

• STIR-FRIED BEANS •
AND PEPPERS WITH
FRIED RICE AND EGGS

Here the egg is stirred into the rice as it cooks so that the rice is flavoured but the egg itself less evident.

The ingredients are the same as in the above recipe for Stir-fried Beans and Peppers with Eggs except that an extra 3 teaspoons soy sauce are needed, making 6 altogether. The method is the same up to the end of stage 4. For 2–3.

• METHOD •

5 Stir the cooked rice in the saucepan with a fork to loosen the grains and ensure that it can be turned quickly into the egg. Place the soy sauce within reach. Warm 2 tablespoons oil over medium heat in the wok or large saucepan. Tilt the wok or large saucepan (unless it is non-stick) so that the oil coats the sides. Pour in the egg, tilt the pan to spread it and as soon as it starts to set add the rice. Stir vigorously from the bottom upwards, breaking up any larger pieces of egg which have set. When all except smaller pieces have disappeared and the rice seems quite dry (which means that the egg is completely cooked), stir in 3 teaspoons soy sauce and remove from the heat. Return the rice to the pan in which it was boiled and cover. Wipe clean or wash the wok or large saucepan.

6 Set the prepared vegetables within easy reach. Heat 3 tablespoons oil in the wok or large pan, add the ginger and allow to fry for a few seconds. Add the onions and fry for another few seconds. Add the pepper and fry, stirring continuously, for 1½–2 minutes. Add the beans and stir-fry for 1 minute. Add the mushrooms and cabbage and stir-fry for 1–2 minutes. Add and stir in another 3 teaspoons soy sauce. Turn the rice and egg into the vegetables, stir thoroughly and serve.

• STIR-FRIED CAULIFLOWER •
WITH PEANUTS AND
SWEET-AND-SOUR SAUCE

Sake (rice wine) has a curious, slightly musky taste, something like retsina with a dash of whisky – or, as someone else has suggested, a mixture of vodka and cold tea. It is neither necessary nor cheap (a bottle will probably cost you £5 or more), but it adds an extra dimension to the sauce in this recipe.

Use small courgettes if possible, because not only do they tend to have more flavour but are firmer-textured.

If you want to save time, start cooking the rice before

blanching the cabbage and cauliflower (in which case, unless you plan to use it the next day, throw away the vegetable water). *For 2–3.*

• INGREDIENTS •

8oz/250 g (2–3 smallish) courgettes

Salt, some of which should be finely ground

8 oz/250 g (½ small) cauliflower

4 oz/125 g (about ¼ small) cabbage

8 oz/250 g brown Patna, American long-grain or Basmati rice

About 3 tablespoons oil

4 oz/125 g Kenya or other stringless green beans

2 cloves garlic

½ inch/1 cm piece fresh root ginger

Juice ½ small lemon

1 dessertspoon honey

2 teaspoons cornflour

3 oz/90 g soft brown sugar

3 tablespoons wine vinegar

2 tablespoons soy sauce (preferably dark)

4 tablespoons sake (optional)

2 oz/50 g cashew nuts

1½ oz/40 g unsalted roasted peanuts

Saucepan with a lid
Wok or large saucepan

• METHOD •

1 Wash the courgettes, peeling off any damaged or discoloured pieces of skin, trim the ends and cut into sticks about ¾ inch/ 2 cm long and ¼ inch/5 mm wide. (The quickest way to do so is to chop the courgettes into ¾ inch/2 cm slices, stand the slices on end and cross-chop. This method is also useful for parsnips and carrots.) Put the slices into a colander, sprinkle with a layer of fine salt and leave to sweat for 30 minutes–1 hour. Rinse under the cold tap and spread on a plate lined with kitchen paper to dry.

2 Wash the cauliflower and cut into florets about ¾ inch/2 cm long and ⅔ inch/1.5 cm across at the flower end. Bring a saucepan containing about ¾ pint/450 ml slightly salted water to the boil, add the cauliflower, bring back to the boil and boil for 2 minutes. Drain in a sieve set over a bowl to catch the cooking water; rinse under the cold tap and leave in the sieve to dry. When you need the sieve for the cabbage, turn the cauliflower on to a plate lined with kitchen paper.

3 Remove any thick stems from the cabbage leaves (by cutting along each side of the stalk with a sharp knife as far as is necessary) and cut the leaves into ½ inch/1 cm squares; wash. Bring about ¾ pint/450 ml salted water to the boil, add the cabbage, return to the boil and boil for 2 minutes. Drain over the bowl of cauliflower water, rinse under the cold tap and leave on a paper-lined plate to dry (you will need to use the sieve when rinsing the rice).

4 Rinse the rice. Put ¾ pint/450 ml of the vegetable water, the rice and a few drops of oil into the saucepan with a lid (no salt is needed as there should be enough in the water already). Bring to the boil, lower the heat, cover and simmer for 30 minutes for Basmati, 30–35 for Patna or American long-grain rice. Test for tenderness by breaking a grain between the thumb and forefinger; if necessary, simmer a few minutes more, adding a little extra water if very dry. Keep covered until you are ready to serve.

5 Top and tail the beans, cut into 1 inch/2.5 cm lengths and wash; leave on another paper-lined plate to dry. Peel and finely slice the garlic. Peel, wipe if necessary and finely slice the ginger, discarding any tough or fibrous pieces.

6 Make the sweet-and-sour sauce. Squeeze the lemon and mix 1 tablespoon of the juice with the honey. Add the cornflour and mix until smooth. Stir in the sugar, vinegar, soy sauce and sake if using it.

7 Check that all the vegetables are dry and blot with more kitchen paper if necessary. Set all the prepared ingredients plus the nuts and sweet-and-sour sauce to hand. Warm 3 tablespoons oil in the wok or large saucepan for a moment or two over high heat. Add the garlic and ginger and allow to fry for a few seconds until just starting to change colour. Add the courgettes and stir-fry for a few seconds. Add the cauliflower and stir-fry for 1 minute. Add the cabbage and stir-fry for 1–2 minutes or until it is cooked but still firm. Add the nuts and stir-fry for a few seconds. Pour in the sauce, stir thoroughly and remove from the heat. Serve on top of the rice.

•VEGETABLE DISHES•

It is hard to give an identity to a chapter on vegetable dishes in a vegetarian cookery book. I intended this to contain recipes based strictly on vegetables rather than on rice, pastry and so on, but in the end it has come to include tofu croquettes, nut burgers and a gratiné dish which is not far removed from a pie.

A main criterion of the recipes has been that they should not be too fussy. There are one or two stuffed dishes, notably Piero's Stuffed Courgettes, but they are very straightforward and do not take nearly as long to prepare as, for instance, cannelloni. One recipe, for marinated kebabs, which might have been included here but which is a little more time-consuming, I have put in the chapter on Parties and Dinner-parties; similarly, there are several recipes for potatoes and a dish using cabbage as the main ingredient in the last chapter of all, for when you are really broke.

•PIERO'S•
STUFFED COURGETTES

With the green courgettes surmounted by gold, cheese-topped stuffing, this looks irresistible; it is also healthy and low in calories since it contains several high-protein ingredients but very little carbohydrate. As it takes only 10 minutes to bake and can be prepared a day ahead, it is especially suitable for evenings when you want a really good meal but expect to arrive home late.

Although it is a stuffed dish, it hardly counts as such in terms of time and fuss as the filling is so firm that it can simply be heaped over the hollowed-out courgette shells. If you do not hollow out the shells very tidily, it will not show; it is preferable to avoid breaking the skins, but even this scarcely matters: just serve carefully. As whole skins are desirable, however, choose vegetables without blemishes. It is also convenient if they weigh 8 oz/250 g or 4 oz/125 g each so that there will be one or two per person. Bigger ones are quicker to prepare but smaller ones usually have more flavour. They should be firm and glossy. The cheapest time to buy courgettes is in the autumn, when British-grown ones are in season. For 4.

• INGREDIENTS •

2 lb/1 kg (preferably 4 or 8) courgettes

Salt, some of which should be finely ground

4 eggs (size 2 or 3)

8 oz/250 g fresh unshelled or 4 oz/125 g frozen peas

1 lb/500 g ripe tomatoes

4 oz/125 g button mushrooms

1 medium onion

3 gloves garlic

1 green chilli

1½ tablespoons olive oil plus a little extra for drizzling

Pepper

2 tablespoons tomato purée

2 oz/50 g Parmesan cheese

Large saucepan
Shallow ovenware dish about 12 inches/30 cm long and 9 inches/23 cm wide

• METHOD •

1 Trim the ends from the courgettes and wash; pare off any brown streaks or blemishes if necessary. Put into the saucepan (you may have to trim a little extra from the ends of large ones to make them fit). Add just enough water to cover and ½ teaspoon salt, bring to the boil and boil 8 oz/250 g courgettes for 11–12 minutes, 4 oz/125 g ones for 8 minutes. Take care to time them, since it is not as easy as with most other vegetables to tell when they are cooked: they should be tender when pricked with a knife, but as they are fairly soft to start with, this is not very helpful. If yours are between the sizes given, you will not go far wrong if you boil them for 10 minutes.

2 Drain the courgettes and leave until they are cool enough to handle. Slice in half lengthways and hollow out the halves by cutting an oblong about ¼ inch/5 mm from the skin along the

sides, ⅓ inch/8 mm deep and ½ inch/1 cm from the ends. Slide the knife gently under the cut section at one end and pull. The flesh (which is the part containing the seeds) generally comes away easily in one strip. Turn the hollowed-out shells upside-down to drain; chop up the strips of flesh and set aside for the filling.

3 Hard-boil the eggs: cover with water, bring to the boil and boil for 12 minutes. Dip into cold water to cool. Shell the peas if necessary, cover with slightly salted water and boil fresh ones for 5–8 minutes or until tender, frozen ones for 3 minutes. Drain.

4 Peel and chop the tomatoes, discarding the hard cores. Trim the stems of the mushrooms, wash, dry and chop fairly finely. Peel and finely chop the onion and garlic. Keep each vegetable separate. Cut off the stalk end of the chilli and discard the seeds and white inner pith. Dice the flesh as finely as possible. Do not rub your eyes while handling it and wash your hands directly afterwards (or wear polythene gloves). Shell and chop the hard-boiled eggs.

5 Fry the onion in the oil over low heat, stirring often, for 8–10 minutes or until soft but not brown. Add the garlic and fry for 3–4 minutes more; add the chilli and turn in the oil; add the mushrooms and continue frying, stirring frequently, for 5–7 minutes. Put in the tomatoes and cook for 7–10 minutes or until liquified, pressing out the lumps of flesh against the sides and bottom of the pan. Season lightly with salt and more moderately with pepper, stir in the tomato purée and continue cooking for 3–4 minutes. Drain the chopped courgette flesh and add with the eggs and peas. Stir and remove from the heat. Unless you are preparing the dish in advance, pre-heat the oven to 400°F, 200°C, Gas Mark 6.

6 Finely grate the Parmesan. Arrange the drained courgette shells (which will have exuded quite a lot of liquid) in the ovenware dish. Spoon the filling over each; as there is a lot, you can pile it quite high. If you are preparing the dish ahead of time, allow the filling to cool, cover with foodwrap and store in the refrigerator until needed. Sprinkle the Parmesan evenly over the top, drizzle with a little extra oil and bake for 10 minutes or until the cheese is crisp and golden. (If you make it in advance, remember that although baking takes only 10 minutes, you will have to allow extra time for the oven to heat.)

·GARLIC MUSHROOMS·

These are *very* garlicky: if you prefer, you can crush one fewer cloves of garlic for the filling, but in my view this spoils part of the point of the dish.

It is very easy to make but presents the problem that the mushrooms have to be cooked in a single layer and, particularly if they are very large, take up too much space to fit into the average large ovenware dish. One answer, obviously, is to use two dishes, but unless you have a fan-assisted oven, which ensures an even distribution of heat from top to bottom, this will mean changing them over at least once during baking or the lower one will cook more slowly. An easier solution is to use a baking-sheet covered with aluminium foil turned up at the edges to catch any liquid (there will not be much, as the mushrooms bake tidily and run little if any surplus juice).

The ideal would be to use very large mushrooms weighing 4 oz/125 g each, so that there would be two per person; slightly smaller ones, however, take up less baking space.

Either the filling or the entire dish (if you have room in the refrigerator) can be prepared a day ahead.

Use stale bread for the breadcrumbs: fresh bread tends to turn into doughy lumps.

Serve with macaroni, pasta shells or polenta. You will need to bake the polenta in advance (see p. 128) and reheat it: put it into the oven when the mushrooms have been cooking for 5–10 minutes. *For 4.*

·INGREDIENTS·

2 tablespoons olive oil

2 lb/1 kg large mushrooms

2 oz/50 g stale wholemeal bread
(weighed without crust)

3 oz/90 g Parmesan cheese

1 medium to large onion

7 medium cloves garlic

Salt

Pepper

1½ oz/40 g butter

Smallish bunch parsley (enough for   5 oz/150 g *medium-fat soft cheese*
   2 tablespoons when chopped)

Baking-sheet

• METHOD •

1 Line the baking-sheet with two layers of aluminium foil. Turn up the edges to make a rim and paint generously with oil. Cut off the mushroom stems; if they are long enough to make it worthwhile, trim the bottoms, wash and chop finely to add to the filling (ignore this if you are making only the filling in advance, as you will not want to prepare the mushroom caps until just before baking). Peel, rinse and dry the caps and lay gill side upwards on the foil – as they will shrink during cooking, it does not matter if they are very close together.

2 Finely grate the bread and the Parmesan. Trim the parsley stalks and wash; blot dry with kitchen paper and chop. Peel and finely chop the onion and 3 of the garlic cloves. Keep each ingredient separate.

3 Fry the onion in the oil over low heat, turning often, for 8–10 minutes or until soft and translucent but not brown; add the chopped garlic and the mushroom stems if you are using them, season lightly with salt and more moderately with pepper and continue frying, turning very frequently, for 5–7 minutes or until the stems are soft and the onion about to change colour. Remove from the heat.

4 Unless you are preparing the dish in advance, pre-heat the oven to 375°F, 190°C, Gas Mark 5. Peel and roughly chop the other 4 cloves of garlic, put into a mortar and crush. Chop the butter into smallish cubes. Add to the mortar with the parsley, ½ teaspoon salt (or a little less if the butter is salted) and a fairly generous sprinkling of pepper. Pound to a paste.

5 Slightly mash the soft cheese with a fork. Add the parsley butter from the mortar, the Parmesan and the contents of the frying-pan, including the oil. Mix thoroughly.

6 Lightly season each mushroom with salt and pepper, spread with a thick layer of filling and top with a generous sprinkling of breadcrumbs. If you have prepared the dish in advance, cool, cover with foodwrap and store in the refrigerator. Bake in the oven for 20–25 minutes or until crisp and well browned.

·STEWED MUSHROOMS·

In particular these are an ideal complement to Clara's Spiced Lentils (see page 97), but they also go very well with Chick Pea and Walnut Burgers (see page 95) and Polenta topped with cheese (see page 128): I stress that the polenta should be with cheese because neither the mushrooms nor plain polenta contains any high-protein ingredient except milk.

You can serve the mushrooms with or without chopped parsley, Croûtons or Garlic Croûtons, according to what they are to accompany. They are also excellent cold with French Dressing (see page 111). For 3–4.

· INGREDIENTS ·

1½ lb/750 g large mushrooms	Salt
5–6 cloves garlic	Pepper
3 tablespoons oil	

TO SERVE (OPTIONAL)

Small bunch parsley or Croûtons and/or Garlic Croûtons (see opposite page) or French Dressing (see page 111)

Large saucepan or wok with a lid

· METHOD ·

1 Trim the mushroom stalks; peel and rinse the mushrooms, wipe dry with kitchen paper and halve or quarter according to size. Cut into slices about ½ inch/1 cm thick. Peel and finely chop the garlic.

2 Fry the garlic in the large saucepan or wok over medium heat for about 30–40 seconds or until it begins to change colour. Add the mushrooms, lower the heat and stir continuously until they have absorbed all the oil. Add 3 tablespoons water, season generously with salt and pepper and turn for about 5 more minutes or until they start to exude liquid. Cover and simmer

for 10 minutes, by which time they will be soft and juicy.

3 If you plan to serve the mushrooms with parsley, trim the parsley stems, wash it, blot dry and chop finely; scatter over the mushrooms and serve at once. Alternatively, if you want to eat the dish cold, dress with salad dressing while still warm and add parsley just before serving. Serve scattered with Croûtons or Garlic Croûtons if you wish.

• CROÛTONS •

If possible, use fairly stale bread, as fresh bread is difficult to cut tidily. For 3–4.

• INGREDIENTS •

*2 slices (about 2 oz/50 g) stale
wholemeal or white bread*

Small baking-sheet

• METHOD •

Pre-heat the oven to 400°F, 200°C, Gas Mark 6. Trim off and discard hard crusts; cut the bread into small cubes. Cover the baking-sheet with aluminium foil, spread the bread cubes on it and bake for 12–15 minutes or until light brown.

• GARLIC CROÛTONS •

• INGREDIENTS •

2 cloves garlic

Butter or margarine for spreading

Salt and pepper

*2 slices (about 2 oz/50 g) stale
wholemeal or white bread*

Small baking-sheet

• METHOD •

Pre-heat the oven to 400°F, 200°C, Gas Mark 6. Peel, roughly chop and crush the garlic. Unless it is already soft, finely chop the butter (if using). Add the butter or margarine to the garlic with a little salt and pepper and beat to mix. Spread over the bread. Trim off and discard hard crusts and cut into small squares. Bake as for Croûtons on page 87.

• CASHEW AND • VEGETABLE GRATIN

Instead of the gratin being on top, as is more usual, in this dish it forms a crisp crust at the bottom, rather like a tart base. The recipe was given at a vegetarian cookery course run by Lynn Cook at Upper Nidderdale, Yorkshire.

You can vary the main vegetables as you wish: leeks and courgettes, as below, are a particularly good combination; another is broccoli and parsnips. Nor do they have to be stir-fried (as broccoli needs blanching before frying, you might as well boil it): it is important, however, to cook them until they are only just tender so that they retain their firmness.

If possible, use stale rather than fresh bread for the bread-crumbs, as fresh tends to form sticky lumps; it is important, however, that they should be freshly grated.

With a larger dish, you will need a little extra sauce: use ¾ pint/450 ml milk, ¾ oz/20 g flour, and another tablespoonful of oil for frying (see step 5).

Allow 30 minutes–1 hour for the courgettes to sweat. For 4–5.

• INGREDIENTS •

8 oz/250 g (2 smallish) courgettes

Salt, some of which should be finely ground

6 oz/190 g stale wholemeal bread

About 4 tablespoons oil

12 oz/375 g (2 large) leeks

4 oz/125 g mushrooms (preferably large)

4 oz/125 g strong Cheddar cheese	Pepper
Small bunch parsley (optional)	2 medium onions
	½ oz/15 g white flour
3½ oz/100 g cashew nuts	½ pint/300 ml milk
5 cloves garlic	Nutmeg

Shallow ovenware dish 8½–10½ in/22–26 cm diameter

• METHOD •

1 Wash the courgettes, trim the ends and pare off any damaged pieces of skin. Chop into sticks about ¾ inch/2 cm long and ¼ inch/5 mm wide (for quick chopping, cut into ¾ inch/2cm lengths and cross-chop). Sprinkle with fine salt and place in a sieve or colander for 30 minutes–1 hour to sweat. Rinse under the cold tap and leave to drain.

2 Make the base. Finely grate the bread; grate the cheese. Trim the stalks of the parsley and wash; blot dry with kitchen paper and chop finely. Roughly chop or crush the nuts. Peel and finely chop 2 cloves of garlic. Mix all the prepared ingredients (except the courgettes) with a moderate seasoning of salt and pepper and 2 tablespoons oil. Lightly oil the dish and press the mixture into a flat layer over the bottom. Pre-heat the oven to 375°F, 190°C, Gas Mark 5. (Since, as with blind-baked quiches, the oven is needed twice, it is more economical not to turn it on until now and to bake the base after preparing the vegetables.)

3 Cut the roots and green leaves from the leeks, peel off the outer layer and discard; wash and slice finely. Place on a plate lined with kitchen paper to drain. Trim the stalks of the mushrooms; peel, rinse and dry large mushrooms or wash and dry buttons. Cut into dice about ½ inch/1 cm square. Peel and finely chop the onions and the remaining 3 cloves of garlic.

4 Put the base into the oven and bake for 15 minutes or until crisp and golden. Check that the leeks and courgettes are dry; blot with kitchen paper if necessary. Set a plate lined with fresh paper to hand. Warm about 1 tablespoon oil in a large frying-pan over high heat. Add some of the garlic, allow to fry for a few seconds until just beginning to change colour and add the courgettes. Stir-fry for 30 seconds. Add the leeks and stir-fry for 2–3 minutes or until soft (the frying may take a little longer than usual with only 1 tablespoon oil). Spread the fried vegetables on the paper-lined plate to drain off surplus oil. Wash or wipe the pan perfectly clean.

5 Fry the onions in the remaining tablespoon of oil over low heat, stirring often, for 8–10 minutes or until soft but not brown. Add the rest of the garlic and fry for 3–4 minutes. Add the mushrooms, season moderately with salt and pepper and continue frying, turning very often, for 5–7 minutes or until soft. (You may need to add a little more oil.) Stir in the flour. As soon as it is absorbed, pour the milk in slowly, stirring continuously, and continue stirring for 3–5 minutes or until it has formed a thick sauce. Add a fairly generous grating of nutmeg, stir in the leeks and courgettes and pour over the cooked base. Return to the oven and bake for 15–20 minutes or until the sauce is beginning to brown.

• HAZELNUT BURGERS •

The possible combinations of ingredients for nut burgers are almost endless. Here my aim has been simply to bring out the rich flavour of the nuts.

The burgers will stick together better if you use a floury potato (such as Maris Piper, Cara or Pentland Squire).

Serve with watercress and/or Tomato Jam (see page 22); if you eat them in buns, sandwich with Tomato Jam and mild cheese such as Edam. *For 4.*

• INGREDIENTS •

8 oz/250 g (1 largish) floury potato	3 cloves garlic
4 oz/125 g (1 medium) parsnip	3½ oz/100 g hazelnuts
4 oz/125 g (2 medium) carrots	3½ oz/100 g walnut pieces
2 sticks celery	2 oz/50 g Parmesan cheese
Salt	2–3 tablespoons oil

Bunch parsley (enough for 3 tablespoons when chopped)	Pepper
1 medium onion	1½ oz/40 g flour

Baking-sheet or large, shallow ovenware dish

• METHOD •

1 Peel the potato, parsnip and carrots. Chop the potato fairly small, cut the parsnip roughly into ½ inch/1 cm cubes and very finely slice or dice the carrots. Cut off the leaf and root ends of the celery, remove any brownish streaks, wash and slice finely. Put the prepared vegetables into a saucepan with a pinch of salt and just enough water to cover, bring to the boil and boil gently for 15–20 minutes or until the potato is soft. Drain and mash (you need only break up the pieces of carrot).

2 Wash the parsley, trim the stalks and blot dry with kitchen paper; chop finely. Peel and finely chop the onion and garlic. Roughly crush the nuts, one sort at a time (a few larger pieces will add textural interest, but if they are too large the burgers will be untidy). Finely grate the cheese.

3 Pre-heat the oven to 400°F, 200°C, Gas Mark 6. Line the baking-sheet or dish with aluminium foil and oil generously. Thoroughly mix all the prepared ingredients with ½ teaspoon salt and a generous sprinkling of pepper. Blend a little salt and pepper into the flour and spread on a plate. Form the mixture into 8 flattish cakes, roll in the flour so that they are generously coated all over and lay them on the foil. Paint all over with oil. Bake in the oven for 25 minutes or until golden-brown.

• TOFU AND •
SPINACH CROQUETTES

Only garlic and Parmesan or pecorino cheese are the equals of smoked tofu as the perfect complement to spinach (the cro-quettes contain garlic but not Parmesan; you do not need both).

The filling or the coated croquettes can be prepared a day in advance. As they take only 15 minutes to bake, this makes them convenient for a quick supper. You can serve them alone or with almost any vegetable: cauliflower, with or without Cheese Sauce (see page 151), or Stewed Mushrooms (page 86) go with them particularly well.

If possible, use stale bread for the crumbs, which should be fine and even – for this reason do not use the crust (which is often difficult to grate).

You could use frozen rather than fresh spinach, but the croquettes will not have so much flavour.

Allow 30 minutes–1 hour for the courgette to sweat. For 3–4.

• INGREDIENTS •

4 oz/125 g (1 smallish) courgette

Salt, some of which should be finely ground

8 oz/250 g spinach

4 oz/125 g stale wholemeal bread (weighed without crust)

3 oz/90 g strong Cheddar cheese

4 oz/125 g mushrooms (preferably button)

6 oz/190 g smoked tofu

3 cloves garlic

Pepper

About 1 tablespoon oil (preferably olive)

4 oz/125 g medium-fat soft cheese

1 oz/25 g wholemeal flour

2 eggs (size 4 or 5)

Saucepan with a lid
Baking-sheet

• METHOD •

1 Trim the ends of the courgette, pare off any damaged or discoloured patches of skin and wash; cut into ¼ inch/5 mm dice (if they are bigger, the croquettes will be untidy). Sprinkle with fine salt and leave in a sieve or colander for 30 minutes–1 hour to sweat. Rinse under the cold tap and blot dry with kitchen paper.

2 Pick over the spinach and wash, twice if necessary. Put into the saucepan with a lid. Add a scant ½ teaspoon salt and 1 tablespoon water. Cover and set over brisk heat for

4–5 minutes; stir and cook for 1–2 minutes more or until submerged in liquid and tender. (For frozen spinach, follow the instructions on the packet.) Drain in a sieve or colander and press out as much liquid as possible. Chop finely.

3 Finely grate the bread, discarding any larger pieces. Grate the Cheddar cheese finely. Trim the stalks of the mushrooms; wash and dry button mushrooms or peel, rinse and dry large ones. Cut into ¼ inch/5 mm dice, as with the courgettes. Drain the tofu if necessary and dice similarly. Peel and finely chop the garlic.

4 Check that the courgette and mushrooms are dry and season lightly with salt and pepper. Warm 1 tablespoon oil in a wok or frying-pan over brisk heat. Add the garlic and fry for a few seconds until it is just beginning to change colour. Add the courgette and stir-fry for 1 minute. Add the tofu and stir-fry for another minute. Add the mushrooms and stir-fry for 1–2 minutes (the stir-frying takes slightly longer than usual with only 1 tablespoon oil). When the mushrooms are soft and the courgette beginning to colour, remove from the heat.

5 Turn the soft cheese into a mixing-bowl and beat with a fork to loosen it. Add the spinach, Cheddar, fried vegetables and 4 tablespoons of the breadcrumbs; mix thoroughly. If you are making the filling in advance, cover and leave to cool. Store in the refrigerator.

6 Pre-heat the oven to 400°F, 200°C, Gas Mark 6. Line the baking-sheet with aluminium foil and oil moderately generously. Season the flour lightly with salt and pepper and spread on a plate. Beat the eggs until smooth, season moderately and pour on to a second plate. Spread out the rest of the breadcrumbs on a third plate. Form the mixture into 10–12 flattened cakes and dip in turn into the flour, egg and breadcrumbs, making sure that they are completely covered but shaking off any surplus each time. Set slightly apart on the baking-sheet. Bake in the oven for 7–8 minutes, then turn and bake for a further 7–8 minutes. Serve hot.

·PULSES·

As I have stated elsewhere in this book, and as you all probably know anyway, pulses are one of the cheapest protein-rich foods available (but remember to eat them with grain). They also have the great advantage that they keep well in the store-cupboard (see pages 12–13); the disadvantage of nearly all beans, however, is the need to soak them before cooking, which means that they cannot be used unless you plan ahead. The one sort of bean which can be boiled straight away is mung, but in compensation it takes a long time to cook; lentils also do not need soaking, and cook much more quickly. I have included a recipe for each of them (Clara's Spiced Lentils and Mung Bean Dal with Lemon) which demands very little else, so that you can prepare an impromptu gourmet meal even though the vegetable rack is bare. You can speed up the soaking time of other pulses by putting them into boiling rather than cold water; they will then be ready to cook in 5–6 hours.

All pulses need boiling fast before simmering: the reason for this is that their skins contain a toxin. In the case of kidney beans you should also change the water. Salt is not usually added until near the end of cooking because it prevents pulses from softening (though with lentils you might add it sooner if you want them to be firm). Simmering in a covered pan helps to prevent the water from evaporating. If you have to add more, use boiling rather than cold.

There are many sorts of pulse besides those for which I have given recipes, notably soya beans, which are exceptional in containing protein which has a high biological value (see page 181). I would have liked to include a dish based on them, but they do not have a particularly interesting flavour and take a very long time to cook. Others include Mexican pinto beans, Italian borlotti beans, black kidney and Brazilian beans, and various kinds of pea.

For quick reference, boiling and simmering times for all those I have used are given below. Simmering times vary, partly according to the freshness of the pulses: those which have been stored for a long time take longer to cook.

	Boiling	*Simmering*
Butter beans	5 minutes	50–60 minutes
Cannellini beans	5 minutes	45–60 minutes
Flageolet beans	5 minutes	45–50 minutes
Haricot beans	5 minutes	40–50 minutes
Kidney beans (red and white)	10 minutes	35–45 minutes
Mung beans	5 minutes	1½ hours
Lentils (green and brown)	2 minutes	30–45 minutes
Chick peas	10 minutes	1–2 hours

•CHICK PEA AND•
WALNUT BURGERS

The idea of these comes from Middle Eastern *falafel*, which are little deep-fried balls made of chick peas and spices.

You can use either ordinary dried chick peas or chick pea flour (available from health-food shops), which gives marginally less flavour but means that you do not have to boil and pound the peas. If you have access to a blender, you can try using it to process the peas: add the given quantity of their liquor, the onion, garlic and cheese. You may, however, find that it sticks because the mixture is too stiff: do not add more liquid. It is also a mistake to include the spices when processing in this way, as they will not be properly ground, or the walnuts, which will make the mixture even stiffer.

It is important to bake the burgers quickly in a hot oven, because if the heat is too low and they take longer, they will become dry. For 4.

• INGREDIENTS •

4 oz/125 g chick peas, soaked
overnight in cold water, or
4 oz/125 g chick pea flour

3½ oz/100 g walnut pieces

2 teaspoons coriander seeds

3 cloves garlic

Salt

4 oz/125 g firm medium-fat
soft cheese

1 *teaspoon cumin seeds*

Small bunch parsley (enough for 2 tablespoons when chopped)

1 *medium to large onion*

About 2 tablespoons oil

1 *oz/25 g wholemeal flour*

Pepper

Small saucepan with a lid
Baking-sheet

• METHOD •

1 If you are using whole chick peas, rinse and pick them over, discarding any which are discoloured, and put into the saucepan with a lid. Add quite a lot of water (but no salt), bring to the boil, boil fast for 10 minutes, cover and simmer for 2½ hours, adding more water as necessary. (This is rather longer than they are usually cooked, but the extra simmering makes them softer and easier to pound.) Drain over a bowl and reserve the cooking liquor. Pound the peas to a paste.

2 Crush the walnuts fairly finely. Crush the coriander and cumin separately from the nuts. Trim the parsley stalks; wash the parsley, blot dry with kitchen paper and chop finely. Peel and finely chop the onion and garlic.

3 Mix together all the prepared ingredients, substituting chick pea flour for the pounded peas if appropriate. Add ½ teaspoon salt, the cheese and 1½ tablespoons of the chick pea liquor or, if you are using flour, water. Work to a stiffish paste.

4 Pre-heat the oven to 425°F, 220°C, Gas Mark 7. Cover the baking-sheet with aluminium foil and grease with 2 tablespoons oil. Season the wholemeal flour with a little salt and pepper and spread on a plate. Mould the mixture into 12–14 small cakes, coat all over with wholemeal flour and set on the baking-sheet. Dribble over a little more oil and bake for 12 minutes. Turn and bake for 5 minutes more or until pale brown. (Do not try to turn earlier, as the burgers may break.)

• CLARA'S SPICED LENTILS •

According to Clara's recipe this is made with harissa, a North African spice mixture consisting chiefly of chillies. Unlike curry powders and garam masala, it is impractical to make at home because a worthwhile quantity entails de-seeding and pulverising a formidable number of chillies; also it keeps for only a few weeks.

You may be able to buy it at a good Italian grocer or delicatessen, but otherwise much the same result is given by adding the equivalent ingredients, as below.

With bought harissa, you could not ask for a simpler recipe, and even without it very little preparation is involved. As it is decidedly hot, however, you need to serve it with something else: when I first had it, at Clara's restaurant, it was accompanied by Stewed Mushrooms (see page 86), which go with it perfectly, but grilled mushrooms or tomatoes are equally suitable. In addition eat it with Rusks (see page 15), Croûtons (see page 87) or hot, crusty bread. *For 3–4.*

• INGREDIENTS •

8 *oz/250 g brown lentils*

Salt

1 *medium onion*

2 *large cloves garlic*

⅓ *inch/8 mm piece cinnamon stick*

1 *teaspoon cumin seeds*

Pepper

1 *teaspoon chilli powder and*
1 *tablespoon harissa or* ⅓ *teaspoon caraway seeds, 3 dried chillies and pinch dried mint*

2 *tablespoons olive oil*

2 *bayleaves*

Saucepan with a lid

• METHOD •

1 Rinse and pick over the lentils, put into the saucepan with a lid and add about 1 pint/600 ml water (but no salt). Bring to the boil, boil fast for 2 minutes, then cover and simmer for 20

minutes or until just soft, adding a pinch of salt towards the end. Drain over a bowl and reserve the cooking liquor.

2 Peel and finely chop the onion. Peel and crush the garlic. Crush the cinnamon and cumin with 1 teaspoon salt and a generous sprinkling of pepper.

3 If you are *not* using harissa, crush the caraway; wash and dry the chillies, trim the stalk ends, slit lengthways, discard the seeds and dice as finely as possible. Do not rub your eyes while chopping the chillies and wash your hands directly afterwards (or wear polythene gloves).

4 Fry the onion in the oil over low heat, turning often, for 8–10 minutes or until soft. Without harissa, turn the chillies in the oil and add the mint, garlic and all the other spices; otherwise add the garlic and spices (including the chilli powder) with the harissa. Fry for 1–2 minutes, turning constantly. Add 8 fl oz/ 225 ml of the lentil liquor, the lentils and the bayleaves and simmer for 20 minutes. If there is still much liquid in the pan, turn up the heat to reduce it until there is just enough to act as a sauce.

• MUNG BEAN DAL • WITH LEMON

Half the point of this is the little crisp chips of fried garlic poured over it just before you eat it; otherwise it is fairly spicy and perceptibly hot, without being fiery.

Mung beans are tiny – hardly bigger than lentils – and, when raw, a particularly fresh, attractive shade of olive green, which unfortunately they lose when cooked. Like lentils they do not need soaking overnight; unlike lentils, however, they take a long time to cook (1½ hours). They are not always sold in supermarkets but can be bought at almost any health-food shop.

As distinct from cooking time, preparation of the dal is quick and easy. Personally I like it simply with hot, crusty bread, but you can add plain grilled mushrooms or tomatoes or serve it with rice. For 3–4.

• INGREDIENTS •

8 oz/250 g (2 medium) onions

¾ inch/2 cm piece cinnamon stick

1 teaspoon cumin seeds

12 oz/375 g mung beans

2 fresh or dried red chillies

3 tablespoons oil

3 teaspoons Jill Norman's Garam Masala (see page 64)

¾ teaspoon salt

Juice 1 small lemon

Handful parsley (enough for 2 tablespoons when chopped)

6 cloves garlic

Wok or large saucepan with a lid

• METHOD •

1 Peel and finely chop the onions. Crush the cinnamon and cumin. Rinse the beans. Wash and dry the chillies; cut off the stalk end, slit lengthways and discard the seeds; dice as finely as possible. Especially with green chillies, do not rub your eyes when handling them and wash your hands directly afterwards (or wear polythene gloves).

2 Put 1 tablespoon of the oil into the wok or large saucepan and fry the onions over low heat, stirring often, for 8–10 minutes or until soft but not brown. Add the chillies and turn in the oil. Add the cumin and cinnamon and continue to fry, stirring constantly, for 1–2 minutes. Add just over 2 pints/1 litre water and the beans. Bring to the boil and boil fast for 5 minutes; reduce the heat, cover and simmer for 45 minutes. Stir in the garam masala and simmer for another 35 minutes. Add the salt and lemon juice. Simmer for 10–15 minutes more or until the beans are very soft. If there is much free liquid in the pan, raise the heat and boil, uncovered, until reduced.

3 Wash, blot dry and finely chop the parsley. Peel and finely slice or chop the garlic. Put the remaining 2 tablespoons of oil into a frying-pan or saucepan and fry the garlic in it over moderate heat until gold rather than brown: it is important not to let it colour too much because it will go on cooking in the hot oil for some seconds off the heat. Serve the dal and add a thick sprinkling of parsley and some of the garlic and oil to each portion.

•CURRIED BEAN CASSEROLE•

This is hot enough to be distinctive without masking the flavour of the ingredients. It is substantial but I have given generous quantities because (unlike some spiced dishes) it keeps its flavour well, so that you can heat up any remains the next day.

Use small button mushrooms which can be left whole to contrast with the texture of the beans.

Serve with hot, crusty bread, not only to combine proteins but also to mop up the sauce. For 4–6.

•INGREDIENTS•

12 oz/375 g red kidney beans, soaked overnight in cold water

3 large sticks celery (outside or near-outside)

Salt

8 oz/250 g button mushrooms

1 red pepper

1½ lb/750 g ripe tomatoes

2 medium onions

4 cloves garlic

1 teaspoon cumin seeds

2 teaspoons coriander seeds

3 dried chillies

3 tablespoons oil

2 teaspoons Jill Norman's Basic Curry Powder (see page 62)

1 teaspoon Jill Norman's Garam Masala (see page 64)

1½ tablespoons tomato purée

1 small lemon

**Wok with a lid, iron-bottomed casserole or large saucepan with a lid
Saucepan with a lid**

•METHOD•

1 Drain and rinse the beans. Put into the saucepan, cover with water (do not add salt), bring to the boil, then skim. Boil fast for 10 minutes. Drain. Return to the pan with fresh water (still

without salt), bring to the boil, reduce the heat, put the lid on the pan and simmer for 25 minutes.

2 Trim the root and leaf ends from the celery, pare off any brownish streaks and wash; cut into slices about ½ inch/1 cm thick. Add to the beans with a little salt when they have simmered for 25 minutes and continue simmering for 10 more minutes or until the beans are tender. Drain over a bowl and keep the cooking liquor.

3 Trim the mushroom stalks, wash the mushrooms and leave on a plate lined with kitchen paper to dry. Wash, dry and quarter the pepper; discard the white inner membrane, seeds and any dark spots and dice. Peel and chop the tomatoes, cutting out the hard cores. Peel and finely chop the onions and garlic. Crush the cumin and coriander seeds. Wash and dry the chillies; remove the stalk ends, slit lengthways, discard the seeds and dice as finely as possible. Do not rub your eyes while chopping them and wash your hands immediately afterwards (or wear polythene gloves).

4 Measure the oil into the wok, casserole or large saucepan with a lid and fry the pepper and onions over low heat, turning often, for 8–10 minutes or until soft. Add the garlic and fry for 3–4 minutes. Add the chillies and turn in the oil. Add the crushed seeds, curry powder and garam masala and fry, turning continuously, for 1–2 minutes. Add the mushrooms and continue to fry, turning constantly, for 5–7 minutes or until soft. Add the tomatoes and simmer for 7–10 minutes, pressing the flesh against the sides and bottom of the pan until liquified. Stir in the tomato purée. Add 8 fl oz/225 ml of the bean liquor and the beans and celery. Wash the lemon and finely grate in the zest. Bring to the boil, cover and simmer for 25 minutes.

• CASSOULET •

The traditional, carnivorous version of cassoulet is a dish of haricot beans accompanied by salted, smoked and other meats. It is cooked very slowly to give the flavours time to permeate and develop, and finished with a gratiné top which contrasts with the creaminess of the beans. In this version the meats are replaced by peppers, tomatoes and a sprinkling of sun-dried tomatoes, which have a much more concentrated flavour than ordinary ones. They are preserved in oil and can be bought loose or in bottles: if in olive oil, they are expensive by any standards, but at the time of writing a 6 oz/190 g jar of sun-dried tomatoes preserved in sunflower oil (of which you will only need half) costs less than £2. If you cannot find (or afford) them, serve the cassoulet with Tomato Jam (see page 22): in this case, however, omit the chillies from the cassoulet recipe, since the jam also contains one and the result would be too hot.

Use firm, glossy peppers and stale bread (fresh bread tends to form doughy lumps when grated into breadcrumbs).

The cassoulet can be made ahead of time – the previous day if you wish. Store overnight in the refrigerator: if necessary, the beans and vegetables can be kept separately, but the flavour will be improved if it is assembled and stored in its casserole.

This is one of the few bean dishes with which there is no need to eat bread, since it is already incorporated: serve with black olives and/or a plain green salad. For 4.

• INGREDIENTS •

12 oz/375 g haricot beans, soaked overnight in cold water

Salt

2 lb/1 kg ripe tomatoes

1 large red pepper

1 large green pepper

3 medium onions

2 fresh or dried red chillies

2–3 tablespoons oil

Pepper

2 teaspoons dried oregano

2 tablespoons tomato purée

4 oz/125 g stale wholemeal bread (weighed without crust)

4 *cloves garlic*   3 *oz/90 g sun-dried tomatoes*

1 *teaspoon cumin seeds*

Saucepan with a lid
Casserole or ovenware dish about 8½ inches/22 cm
in diameter and 3½–4 inches/9–10 cm deep

• METHOD •

1 Drain and rinse the beans. Put into the saucepan with a lid and cover with fresh cold water; do not add salt. Bring to the boil and boil fast for 5 minutes, then lower the heat, cover and simmer for 35 minutes. Add a little salt and continue to simmer for 10 minutes more or until the beans are tender. Drain over a bowl and keep the cooking liquor.

2 Peel and chop the fresh tomatoes. Wash and quarter the peppers, remove the cores and all the seeds and trim off the white inner membrane and any dark spots on the red one; cut the flesh into strips. Peel the onions and cut into fine rings. Peel and finely chop the garlic. Crush the cumin. Wash and dry the chillies; trim the stalk ends, remove the seeds and dice as finely as possible. Do not rub your eyes while chopping them and wash your hands directly afterwards.

3 Fry the onions and peppers in the oil over low heat for 20 minutes or until soft; turn frequently, particularly towards the end. Add the garlic and fry for 2–3 minutes. Add the chillies and cumin and fry for 2–3 minutes more. Add the fresh tomatoes, season lightly with salt and fairly generously with pepper and simmer for 7–10 minutes, pressing out the lumps of flesh against the sides and bottom of the pan. Sprinkle in the oregano and stir in the tomato purée. Simmer for 15 minutes. Stir in 3½ fl oz/100 ml of the reserved bean water.

4 Pre-heat the oven to 300°F, 150°C, Gas mark 2. Finely grate the bread. Roughly chop the dried tomatoes. Put half the beans into the bottom of the casserole. Cover with half the vegetables and sprinkle with the dried tomatoes. Add the rest of the beans and vegetables. Spread the breadcrumbs in a thick layer over the top and bake in the oven for 1–1½ hours. If the breadcrumbs have not coloured, turn up the oven to 375°F, 190°C, Gas Mark 5, for a few minutes to brown them.

·EGGS·

I am taking it absolutely for granted that everyone who reads this book will use free-range eggs, or at least avoid battery-produced ones. The regulations governing free-range hens point to a very reasonable life: they must have continuous access to open-air runs, most of which should be covered with grass or other vegetation, and are guaranteed a minimum of 10 square metres of space each (10 square metres is about the area of a small bedroom).

In addition to free-range are three other classes of non-battery rearing, 'semi-intensive', 'deep litter' and 'barn'. The first is the same as free-range but the hens have only a quarter as much space per head; 'deep litter' means that they are kept indoors, with straw or some other litter material over at least part of the floor, at a density of seven hens per square metre, which gives them enough space to move about but is pretty crowded; 'barn' is the same but with extra perching space and a density of 25 hens per square metre. Eggs produced by these methods should be correspondingly labelled.

The problem of salmonella infection has been tackled by a series of precautions at different levels: factories producing feed are inspected more often than before and output tested daily; all laying flocks are monitored and destroyed if salmonella is found, and sales of suspect poultry and eggs restricted. Nevertheless, official advice from the Ministry of Agriculture, Fisheries and Food is that anyone vulnerable (children, the old and the infirm) should avoid eggs which have not been heated sufficiently to kill bacteria – that is, until set. Although these categories are unlikely to include readers of this book, the eggs are in fact cooked until set in all recipes: this may seem over-careful, but anyone who has had salmonella will see the point. Further precautions are to wash eggs before cracking and your hands and utensils used for them while raw as soon as possible after preparing them.

Having said this, I should emphasise that eggs are a wonderful food: high in protein and minerals, low in calories, quick to cook – and, even at free-range prices, remarkably cheap.

•OEUFS FLORENTINE•

This is a classic dish of spinach, eggs and cheese sauce which ideally you would make by breaking the raw eggs directly into the spinach and baking them under the sauce. The snag is that baked eggs are unsatisfactory unless the yolks are still runny, which, apart from the risk of salmonella infection, means that the sauce does not have time to brown. The second problem can be solved by cooking the dish under the grill rather than in the oven; the following method, however, is easier and safer.

Do not be tempted to use Swiss chard, sea-kale beet or the New Zealand variety instead of real spinach in this recipe. When possible, choose fresh spinach sold on the root. If the only option is frozen, use leaf rather than chopped and follow the cooking instructions on the packet. *For 4.*

• INGREDIENTS •

1 *lb/500 g spinach*	1 *bayleaf*
Salt	4 *eggs (size 2 or 3)*
4 *cloves garlic*	2 *oz/50 g Gruyère or*
1¼ *oz/30 g butter*	*Cheddar cheese*
2 *tablespoons oil*	2 *oz/50 g Parmesan cheese*
(preferably olive)	¾ *oz/20 g flour*
¾ *pint/450 ml milk*	Pepper

Large saucepan with a lid
Shallow ovenware dish about 12 x 8½ inches/30 x 22 cm

• METHOD •

1 Tear the spinach leaves from the roots and/or pick them over, discarding any which are damaged. Wash, twice if necessary. Pack into the saucepan with a lid, add 1 tablespoon water and ½ teaspoon salt, cover and set over medium heat for 4 minutes. Stir and continue to cook for 1–2 more minutes or until

the spinach is submerged in juice and tender. Drain and press out surplus water with the back of a spoon.

2 Peel and finely chop the garlic. Melt ½ oz/15 g of the butter in 1 tablespoon of the oil over medium heat and fry the garlic for about 30 seconds or until just starting to change colour. Remove the pan from the heat and add the spinach. Toss until thoroughly mixed. Spread the spinach mixture over the bottom of the ovenware dish and make 4 indentations in it for the eggs to sit in.

3 Heat but do not boil the milk with the bayleaf. Cover and set aside. Boil the eggs for 6 minutes. Drain the hot water from the saucepan, leaving the eggs inside, and refill briefly with cold water to cool them. Then shell carefully and place in the indentations in the spinach.

4 Pre-heat the oven to 400°F, 200°C, Gas Mark 6. Coarsely grate the Gruyère or Cheddar and the Parmesan separately. Make the cheese sauce. Melt the rest of the butter in the remaining tablespoon of oil, add the flour and stir until amalgamated; be careful not to let it brown. Remove the bayleaf from the milk and discard. Pour the milk slowly into the fat and flour mixture, stirring continuously; keep stirring until the sauce has thickened. Season lightly with salt and more generously with pepper and simmer for 5–6 minutes. Remove from the heat and stir in the Gruyère or Cheddar and about half the Parmesan. Pour over the eggs and spinach. Scatter the rest of the Parmesan over the top. Bake in the oven for 15–20 minutes or until the sauce is golden and bubbling.

• PIERO'S MACARONI •
AND GOAT'S CHEESE
OMELETTE

You might think that stuffing an omelette with macaroni was just a way of making it more filling. The result is certainly hefty and satisfying, but that is not the reason for its inclusion here. All I will say is – try it.

You need a full-flavoured cheese, though it need not taste distinctively of goat. I particularly recommend plain log (*boucheron*) or Chèvre du Berry.

Very little preparation is needed and if you use quick-cooking macaroni, which takes only 7–8 minutes to boil, the omelette (or at least, the first omelette) can be on the table in 15 minutes. Serve with a green salad tossed in French Dressing (see page 111). *For 4 (makes 2 omelettes).*

• INGREDIENTS •

4 oz/125 g thin-cut macaroni	*8 eggs (size 2)*
Salt	*Pepper*
About ½ oz/15 g butter	*2 tablespoons oil (preferably olive)*
8 oz/250 g goat's cheese	

Fish-slice

• METHOD •

1 Boil the macaroni in plenty of slightly salted water according to the instructions on the packet. Drain and immediately toss with the butter (this will prevent the pieces from sticking together).

2 Trim the rind from the cheese and chop or crumble it into small pieces. Break the eggs into 2 bowls (1 for each omelette). Season fairly generously with salt and pepper and beat with a fork until smooth.

3 Heat 1 tablespoon of the oil over medium heat. Pour in the first set of eggs. Tilt the pan so that the egg runs to the bottom and sets; fold back the set part and continue to tip so that more egg runs to the bottom. Repeat until there is no more liquid. Immediately distribute half the macaroni over the egg. Spread half the cheese over the macaroni. As soon as the top layer of egg is set (test it by prodding gently under the cheese) and the bottom of the omelette golden (lift the corner with the fish-slice to check) fold it carefully in half. Remove from the heat, cut into two and serve. Wash or thoroughly wipe the pan and repeat for the second omelette.

• PIPERADE •

This looks much better if the eggs are cooked less, but this means that they have not been sufficiently heated to kill bacteria.

Choose firm, shiny peppers. Serve with plenty of warm, crusty bread. For 2–3.

• INGREDIENTS •

1 lb/500 g ripe tomatoes	2 tablespoons olive oil
1 large red pepper	Salt
1 large green pepper	Pepper
8 oz/250 g (2 medium) onions	1 generous tablespoon tomato purée
4 large cloves garlic	4 eggs (size 2)

• METHOD •

1 Peel and roughly chop the tomatoes, discarding the hard cores. Wash, dry and quarter the peppers; remove the cores, white inner membranes and all the seeds (which are hot) and cut out any dark spots; dice the flesh fairly finely. Peel the onions and slice into thin rings. Peel and finely chop the garlic.

2 Fry the onions and peppers in the oil over low heat for 15–20 minutes or until thoroughly soft, turning often, especially towards the end (watch the green pepper in particular to ensure that it does not blacken). Add the garlic and continue to fry for 3–4 minutes. Add the tomatoes, season with ⅔ teaspoon salt and a generous dusting of pepper and cook for another 5 minutes. Stir in the tomato purée and simmer for 15–20 minutes or until thick.

3 Break the eggs into a bowl, season moderately and beat with a fork until smooth. Pour into the peppers and tomatoes, then tilt the pan so that they run to the bottom and set; fold the set part back into the vegetables and repeat until no liquid is left. Stir the fragments of egg gently into the sauce and cook for another 4–5 minutes. Serve at once.

· SCRAMBLED EGGS WITH · CHEESE AND CHIVES

A particular advantage of eggs is speed of cooking: indeed, my chief reason for including this recipe is that you can prepare it in scarcely more time than it takes to make plain scrambled eggs.

However, the taste of the chives is important, which means that if you do not grow them (or if it is winter) the dish cannot be made on the spur of the moment. The flavour of the cheese also counts: use a fresh-tasting one such as ricotta.

Serve with crusty bread or toast (make toast before you start cooking the eggs).

· INGREDIENTS ·

PER PERSON

Small bunch chives (enough for 1 heaped dessertspoon when chopped)

2 eggs (size 2 or 3)

Salt

Pepper

1½ oz/40 g ricotta or other fresh-tasting medium-fat soft cheese

½ oz/15 g butter

· METHOD ·

1 Trim the stems of the chives. Wash, blot dry with kitchen paper and chop finely.
2 Beat the eggs until smooth with a generous seasoning of salt and pepper. Soften the cheese with a fork if necessary.
3 Melt the butter in a small saucepan over low heat. Pour in the eggs and stir continuously from the bottom upwards until creamy, lumpy and almost set, as for ordinary scrambled eggs. Remove from the heat and stir in the cheese gently until it has melted: this will make the mixture runny. Add the chives and return to the heat for 1–1½ minutes or until it has returned to the consistency of plain scrambled egg. Eat at once.

·SALADS·

'A salad a day keeps the doctor away' is rather a vague statement, as a salad can be made of almost anything: if it includes at least a little raw produce, however, I firmly believe it, since raw fruit and vegetables as nearly as possible retain all their nutrients – I say as nearly as possible because they start to lose vitamin C as soon as they are cut. It is not only for this reason, but also because crispness and flavour progressively deteriorate after harvesting, that freshness really counts. In general it is a better idea to buy whatever seems freshest and to plan your salad round it than to decide what you want in advance.

As the case of tomatoes illustrates, however, freshness is not the only factor which determines flavour. The taste of tomatoes has suffered in the interests of quantity. The same has happened to lettuces. As one retailer puts it, the flavour of the popular varieties has been grown out of them. Partly to counter this, the supermarkets are offering an increasing choice of the less usual kinds, for example, frisée, endive, batavia, lamb's lettuce, Butterhead and Wallop (which are traditional but until recently ignored English varieties) and several sorts of red lettuce such as Lollo Rosso, oakleaf and radiccio. Of these the most reliable in terms of flavour are probably the last two, which are respectively slightly and distinctly bitter. There are also crisp, sweet Cos and the similar but tiny Little Gem. Organically grown lettuces often also have flavour, but not always; more consistent are organic spinach and carrots, which in my experience are generally delicious.

Obviously organic produce is preferable on other grounds, particularly with regard to pesticides, which you cannot remove. For better or worse, cooking may break down some of their components but will not dissipate them; washing only cleans off surface residues – although this helps. When possible, scrub items and rinse in running water to clear off the soapy spray with which pesticides are applied.

Consistently with my condemnation of the majority of lettuces, I have excluded them from the recipes which follow, not because I suggest avoiding them altogether but because I recommend the more expensive sorts and feel that to use these merely as background to a mixed salad does not give the best value for money. An oakleaf or Cos or (for 4) a pair of Little Gem will cost at least two-thirds more than an ordinary round summer or hot-house lettuce: to appreciate them as they deserve, serve them as a side vegetable alone or, in the case of radiccio, with other leaves. Add just chives or spring onions plus French Dressing to Cos, Little Gem or oakleaf; mix radiccio, which is chewy and stronger, with spinach and the inner leaves of a green cabbage. In winter buy watercress and a couple of heads of chicory rather than lettuce: if you want more, try a sliced orange instead of tomatoes.

The recipes should be looked on merely as examples: give precedence to freshness and compose your own according to the ingredients available. Bear in mind, however, that not only flavour but also texture and, perhaps more than with any other type of dish, eye appeal play their part: try to contrast colours and arrange the ingredients not necessarily too carefully but interestingly. Wash (but do not cut) salad greens well in advance to give them time to drain, but do not add dressing until just before serving or they may become limp. Chicory can be chopped or the leaves left whole (slice the centres in half); tear lettuces into bite-sized pieces.

The flavour of olive oil really matters in a salad dressing. Similarly, use wine as opposed to malt vinegar. Low-fat Lemon and Tomato Dressing is a useful alternative to French if you prefer to consume (or use) less oil.

All the salads in this chapter are substantial enough to serve as a main course.

• FRENCH DRESSING •

• INGREDIENTS •

4 *tablespoons olive oil*	Salt
1 *tablespoon wine vinegar* (*red or white*)	Pepper

• METHOD •

Beat together the oil and vinegar with a fork and season with salt and pepper. As oil and vinegar do not amalgamate but separate out, beat the dressing again just before serving.

• LEMON AND •
TOMATO DRESSING

• INGREDIENTS •

8 oz/250 g ripe tomatoes	Salt
1 small lemon	Pepper
1 tablespoon olive oil	

• METHOD •

Peel, chop and sieve the tomatoes, pressing as much flesh through the sieve as you can (they are very difficult to liquify unless you skin them first). Squeeze the lemon juice and add with the oil. Season lightly with salt and pepper and beat with a fork.

• YOGHURT CHEESE •
DRESSING

• INGREDIENTS •

4 tablespoons Yoghurt Cheese (see page 180)	4 tablespoons olive oil
	1½ tablespoons wine vinegar

• METHOD •

Soften the cheese with a fork. Mix together the oil and vinegar and beat gradually into the cheese (do not add the cheese to

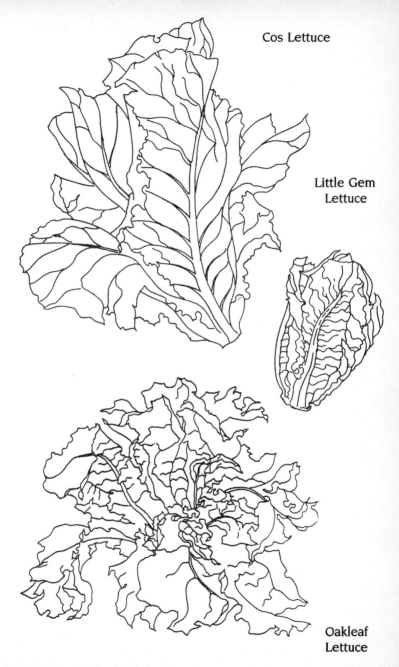

Cos Lettuce

Little Gem
Lettuce

Oakleaf
Lettuce

the oil). Beat as smooth as possible. The dressing should be very thick. If left to stand, it may separate slightly: beat again with a fork before serving.

•YOGHURT DRESSING•

• INGREDIENTS •

4 *tablespoons olive oil*

1½ *tablespoons wine vinegar*

8 *oz/250 g Greek or other plain yoghurt (if you use sharp yoghurt, you may need extra sugar)*

Salt

Pepper

About ½ teaspoon soft brown sugar

• METHOD •

Mix together the oil and vinegar. Beat gradually into the yoghurt (do not add the yoghurt to the oil: thick-set yoghurt may not blend). Season lightly with salt and pepper and add sugar to taste.

•GREEK SALAD•

For the whole of a holiday on one of the less popular Greek islands (Samos, just off the coast of Turkey) I had this salad every day, not from choice but because very little food was imported and at that time of the year the only ingredients in season were onions, cucumbers and tomatoes. Chiefly because the tomatoes were so delicious, I did not become tired of it, but, on the contrary, have since often made the nearest approximation possible in this country. The tomatoes were huge and, because of the sun, sweet and squashy on one side and greenish on the other, so that each one was almost like two different sorts of fruit. They were served in thick, wedge-shaped slices; the cucumbers were peeled and roughly chopped, and thick rings of red or white onion were scattered over the top of the salad. The other ingredients were olives and Greek Feta cheese sprinkled with thyme (the whole island smelt of thyme). As is usual in Greece, dressing was not served but olive oil and slices of lemon were left on the table.

If you can find large Mediterranean tomatoes, which are irregularly shaped and slightly ribbed, use them (but do not substitute the large, smooth, so-called 'beefsteak' variety, which are not at all the same). Red onions are slightly milder than the usual kind; they are a deep, purplish red which happens to go particularly well with the red of tomatoes. If you cannot get fresh thyme, omit the herb completely: dried thyme will just taste gritty.

The salad is as near instant as you can get: because simplicity is part of its character, do not worry too much about presentation. Serve with hot bread. *For 4.*

• INGREDIENTS •

1¼–1½ lb/625–750 g
Mediterranean or firm ordinary
tomatoes

8 inch/20 cm piece cucumber

2 onions (preferably red)

A few sprigs fresh thyme

12 oz–1 lb/375–500 g
Greek Feta cheese

4 oz/125 g black olives

1 lemon

Olive oil

Salt

Pepper

• METHOD •

1 Wash the tomatoes and chop into thick wedges or slices, discarding the hard cores. Wash or peel the cucumber and cut into chunks. Peel and coarsely chop or thickly slice the onions. Wash the thyme, blot dry with kitchen paper and pull the leaves from the stems.

2 Cut the cheese into 4 slabs and place in 4 serving-bowls or on plates. Sprinkle with the thyme. Put the tomato and cucumber round or over it. Scatter the onion on top and stud with the olives. Quarter the lemon and serve separately with the oil, salt and pepper.

• MICHAEL'S TOMATO AND •
MOZARELLA SALAD

As made by Michael, this is one of the most picturesque salads I have ever seen. He puts the white cheese in the centre of the plate and surrounds it with a dark green circle of beans and basil; next comes a circle of orange-red tomatoes strewn with reddish-purple onion and black olives, and round the outside is a final circle of bright green pepper.

The salad is relatively expensive, but will be cheaper if you use green haricot rather than French or Kenya beans; this applies especially in the autumn, when British-grown haricots are in season.

Choose smooth, glossy peppers and firm beans: if the peppers are wrinkled or the beans floppy, they are old. *For 4.*

• INGREDIENTS •

1 lb/500 g haricot, Kenya, or other stringless green beans

1¼–1½ lb/625–750 g firm tomatoes

2 green peppers

2 onions (*preferably red*)

10–12 basil leaves

12 oz/375 g mozarella cheese

4 oz/125 g black olives

French Dressing (*see page* 111)

• METHOD •

1 Wash and top and tail the beans and cut into shortish lengths. Just cover with slightly salted water, bring to the boil and boil for 5–6 minutes or until just tender but still firm. Drain and leave to cool.

2 Wash and dry the tomatoes and peppers. Slice the tomatoes into rings, discarding the stalk ends. Halve the peppers, remove the white inner membrane, cores and all the seeds and slice the flesh fairly thinly. Peel and coarsely chop the onions. Wash the basil leaves and blot dry with kitchen paper.

3 Drain the mozarella (which is packed in whey to keep it

moist) and slice thickly. Place the slices in the centre of 4 serving-plates. Arrange the beans in a ring round the cheese. Set the slices of tomato in a ring round the beans and the strips of pepper outside the tomatoes. Strew the tomatoes with the pieces of onion and dot with olives. Cut the basil into narrow strips and scatter over the beans. Just before serving, beat the dressing with a fork and pour some over each portion.

•COTTAGE CHEESE AND• FRUIT SALAD

Once you have tried this, you will never be tempted by its faint-hearted imitators in the form of commercial cottage cheese flavoured with fruit again. It is not only wonderfully refreshing on a hot day, but healthy, low-calorie (one of its advantages is that it does not need dressing), and also quicker than the average salad to prepare; nor need the fruit cost much more than the equivalent salad vegetables.

To a greater extent than usual it is an idea rather than a hard-and-fast recipe. The idea comes from one of the café/restaurants owned by the fashion retailer Joseph, where the fruit tends to include the most exotic available (such as star-fruit), but any kinds which go with the cheese are suitable, and most do: the only common one which seems to me to jar is the orange. Of those given below, the least dispensable are the passion fruit and banana.

Passion fruit (or grenadilloes) are small, round, dark brown fruits, the skin of which crinkles as they ripen. In contrast to their unpromising exterior appearance, however, the flesh (if it can be called that) is ringed with delicate red and has a peculiar but delicious scent. They are full of little pips, which you eat: as the flesh is almost liquid, you need a teaspoon. They are becoming increasingly easy to buy, and, at least relatively, are extremely cheap. Kiwi fruit are also fairly cheap; rosy grapefruit are considerably more expensive than the ordinary kind but you may prefer their sweeter, more delicate flavour. For 4.

• INGREDIENTS •

8 oz/250 g grapes
(seedless are quicker to prepare)

4 firm tomatoes or 8 oz/250 g
cherry tomatoes

1 ordinary or rosy grapefruit

2 kiwi fruit

2 bananas

1 apple

A few drops lemon juice

1½ lb/750 g plain cottage cheese

Salt

Pepper

2 passion fruit

• METHOD •

1 Wash the grapes and blot dry with kitchen paper; halve them and take out the pips if necessary. Wash or peel the tomatoes and remove stalks.

2 Peel the grapefruit: to remove all the pith, do not pull off the skin but use a sharp knife. Chop or slice the flesh, discarding the pips, and put a quarter of it in a neat heap on the side of each of 4 plates. Peel the kiwi fruit (again using the knife), trim the stalk end and slice; arrange on the side of each plate opposite the grapefruit. Peel and slice the bananas and place between the grapefruit and kiwi fruit. Wash, quarter, core and chop the apple, sprinkle with a little lemon juice to prevent it from going brown and set next to the banana. Arrange the grapes and tomatoes in the gaps between the other fruit so that all but an empty space in the middle of each plate is filled.

3 Season the cottage cheese with salt and pepper to taste. Wash and halve the passion fruit. Place a half in the centre of each plate. Surround with the cheese and serve.

• TUSCAN-STYLE BEAN AND •
TOMATO SALAD

This is an adaptation of an Italian country recipe, Tuscan bread salad, which is a kind of bread and vegetable pâté. It is the most refreshing salad I know on a hot day.

Flageolet beans, because they are picked before they are ripe, are lighter and milder in flavour than other sorts of dried bean. You may not be able to buy them at your local supermarket, but they will be stocked at almost any health-food shop. The salad is clearer-tasting and looks more attractive if made with white rather than brown bread: brown dulls the pink of the tomato juice. *For 4.*

• INGREDIENTS •

*4 oz/125 g flageolet beans,
soaked overnight in cold water*

Salt

*2 lb/1 kg ripe tomatoes and
4 firm tomatoes*

*8–10 oz/250–310 g bread
(weighed without crust)*

2 large green peppers

2 medium onions

2 tablespoons oil

2 tablespoons vinegar

Pepper

12–16 basil leaves (optional)

Small saucepan with a lid

• METHOD •

1 Drain and rinse the beans. Cover with fresh cold water in the small saucepan (do not add salt). Bring to the boil, skim and boil fast for 5 minutes. Reduce the heat, cover and simmer for 35 minutes, then add a little salt and simmer for 10–15 more minutes or until tender. Drain.

2 Skin, fairly finely chop and sieve the ripe tomatoes (sieve half at a time). It may sound silly to suggest skinning them prior to sieving, but they are otherwise almost impossible to liquify. Cut the bread into smallish pieces and put to soak in the juice.

3 Wash and quarter the peppers, discarding the cores, white inner membrane and seeds (which are hot) and finely dice the flesh: the pieces should resemble peas in size. Peel and finely chop the onions. Stir both into the bread and tomato juice. Add the beans, oil, vinegar, ½ level teaspoon salt and a moderate sprinkling of pepper and mix gently.

4 Wash and dry the firm tomatoes and cut each one into 8 segments. If you are using basil, wash it and shake or blot dry.

Turn the salad mixture into 4 serving-bowls, arrange the tomato segments round the edge and place 3 or 4 basil leaves in the centre of each.

•CARROT AND PEANUT SALAD•

Although this is particularly good made with fine-textured, little, new carrots, older ones are also suitable: the important point is that they should have plenty of flavour. If you can, buy organic ones, since in my experience carrots usually have more flavour when grown in this way.

The salad does not take long to prepare except for chopping the carrots, which, as the aim is to match the size of the peanuts, should be cut up fairly small.

Tiny new carrots can simply be sliced; the quickest method of chopping bigger ones is to slice them and then cross-chop several slices at a time.

This salad goes particularly well with Baked Potatoes (see page 167). For 4.

• INGREDIENTS •

1 lb/500 g carrots

2 bunches spring onions

8 oz/250 g sultanas

8 oz/250 g unsalted peanuts

French or Lemon and Tomato Dressing (see pages 111 and 112)

4 crisp apples

• METHOD •

1 Trim the ends of the carrots and peel or scrub and dry them. Slice new ones or slice and cross-chop others into ⅓ inch/8 mm dice. Cut the root and green leaves from the onions, peel off the outer layer and (since they are otherwise too slippery to chop easily) slide off the fine membrane underneath and discard; chop the onions fairly finely.

2 Separate any sultanas which have stuck together. Put the carrots, onions, sultanas and peanuts into a salad bowl. Pour the dressing over them. Wash, quarter, core and finely chop the apples; add to the salad and toss.

• POTATO AND •
CUCUMBER SALAD

The portions in this recipe are large: if you are serving something else as well, I suggest making only half the quantity.

Use waxy, preferably new potatoes, such as Pentland Javelin, Ulster Sceptre or Maris Bard.

Although the end result looks less tidy, I personally much prefer unpeeled potatoes in a salad.

If you want to peel them, however, do it after they are cooked, when the skin will peel off easily rather as with tomatoes: this will give a neater result than peeling them raw and has the advantage of retaining vitamin C, which in potatoes is concentrated under the skin.

If fresh dill is unobtainable, use a spear of mint. *For 4.*

• INGREDIENTS •

2 lb/1 kg waxy potatoes	*8 inch/20 cm piece cucumber*
Salt	*8 eggs*
Double quantity French Dressing (see page 111)	*Small bunch dill*

• METHOD •

1 Scrub the potatoes, put into a saucepan, just cover with water and add ⅓ teaspoon salt. Boil for 15–18 minutes or until just tender. Slice them as soon as they are cool enough to handle and place in a salad bowl. Cover with the dressing.

2 Wash and dry the cucumber. Cut into small dice (slice and cross-chop). Sprinkle with a little salt and leave to drain in a sieve until just before you are ready to serve.

3 Boil the eggs for 12 minutes. Drain the water from the saucepan, leaving the eggs behind, and refill with cold water to cool them. Then shell the eggs, slice them and put them into the salad bowl with the potatoes. Toss gently so that they too are covered with dressing.

4 Spread the cucumber in a thick layer over the eggs and potatoes. Wash the dill and blot dry with kitchen paper. Pull the leaves (which are like hairs) from the central stem and chop finely. Sprinkle over the cucumber.

• AVOCADO AND •
ALMOND SALAD

This was invented by Michael as an alternative to avocado and grapefruit salad, which is delicious but, as it is just what its name indicates and no more, hardly constitutes a meal. This salad, however, looks extremely elegant and is much more satisfying than its size suggests.

If possible, use blood rather than ordinary oranges, as they look more picturesque and are sharper. It is important to use oranges with good flavour, but the only other guidance I can give is to choose small rather than large ones.

The avocadoes should 'give' slightly all over when gently pressed: if they are hard, they are underripe. (They will ripen in a few days if left at room temperature.) Avoid any which are very soft or have soft patches.

The salad will be enormously improved if you crisp the nuts. The best method is to bake them in the oven, but if it has to be heated specially it is more economical to toast them in a saucepan. For 4.

• INGREDIENTS •

Salt	2 *avocado pears*
3½ oz/100 g *whole almonds*	French Dressing (*see page* 111)
1 *lb*/500 g *medium-fat soft cheese*	2 *blood or other sharp oranges*

Small baking-sheet (optional)

• METHOD •

1 If you are going to crisp the almonds in the oven, pre-heat it to 400°F, 200°C, Gas Mark 6, and line the baking-sheet with aluminium foil. Sprinkle just a very little salt over the almonds, spread them over the baking-sheet and bake for 5–6 minutes. Alternatively put them into a thick saucepan and toast over high heat for 3–4 minutes, shaking constantly to ensure even cooking. Allow to cool and roughly chop.

2 Divide the cheese into 4 portions and set in the middle of the serving-plates. Halve the avocados, remove the stones and any dark spots or streaks and peel away the skin. Cut each half across into thin, crescent-shaped slices. Place in a circle round the cheese and pour the dressing over them.

3 Peel the oranges: do not pull off the skin, which will leave pith, but use a sharp knife. Cut the flesh horizontally into fairly thin slices, discarding all the pips and reserving any juice which escapes during cutting. Halve the slices and arrange over the avocado. Pour the juice over them. Scatter the nuts over the cheese and serve.

• COLESLAW •

Coleslaw stands or falls according to its dressing: obviously, really crisp, fresh vegetables are also necessary, but without the contrast of a rich, creamy dressing they lose some of their impact. As the salad includes a number of sweet ingredients (carrots, mange-tout peas, apples, walnuts and raisins) the dressing also needs to be slightly sharp. The one I recommend is based on Yoghurt Cheese: I have given the alternative of an ordinary Yoghurt Dressing, but it does not have quite the same richness and depth. It is not essential but a great improvement to crisp the nuts. *For 3–4.*

• INGREDIENTS •

3½ oz/100 g *walnut pieces*

8 oz/250 g *white cabbage*

2 oz/50 g *raisins*

1 *crisp apple*

2 sticks celery

2 oz/50 g mange-tout peas

4 oz/125 g carrots

1 medium onion

Yoghurt Cheese Dressing
(see page 113) or
Yoghurt Dressing (see page 114)

Small baking-sheet or thick saucepan (optional)

• METHOD •

1 Crisp the nuts. Either cover the baking-sheet with aluminium foil, spread them over it and bake for 5 minutes in a pre-heated oven at 400°F, 200°C, Gas Mark 6, or shake them in a thick saucepan over high heat for 1½–2 minutes – shake almost continuously after the first minute, since they burn very easily. (The nuts may stain the saucepan slightly pink, but this soon wears off: much more important is that it should be thick, as dry-toasting will make it very hot.) Chop the nuts slightly: unless the pieces are bigger than usual, very little chopping is needed.

2 Discard the outermost leaves of the cabbage and cut into slices from one side. Wash the slices, shake in a sieve and set on a plate lined with kitchen paper to dry. Chop into pieces about ½ inch/1 cm long.

3 Cut the leaf and root ends from the celery, peel off and discard any brownish streaks, wash and leave on a plate lined with kitchen paper to dry; slice finely. Trim the stalk ends of the peas, wash, dry and cut into strips about ¼ inch/5 mm across. Scrub or peel the carrots, trim the ends and finely slice. Peel and finely chop the onion.

4 Put all the prepared ingredients into the salad bowl. Separate the raisins if necessary and add. Wash, quarter and core the apple; chop into ½ inch/1 cm dice. Add the apple to the salad with the dressing, toss thoroughly and serve.

·BREAD, SCONES·
MUFFINS AND CAKES

In compiling this chapter I have been influenced by two schools of thought: one maintains that since cakes (as opposed to bread) are unnecessary and unhealthy, they should not be included in a book of this kind; the other, more hedonistically (realistically?), argues that, as people are going to eat cakes anyway, they are better off making their own than buying them. I have therefore divided the recipes equally between the two: the first four recipes are useful and the rest indulgent. In describing the earlier items as useful I am not doing them justice, for few things are more delicious than wholemeal bread straight from the oven or a creamy polenta; the scones and muffins are useful in that they are cheap, very quick to make and either positively or relatively healthy (the scones contain cheese and the muffins less than half the usual proportion of fat and sugar in cakes). I have deliberately chosen items for the second half which include nuts; beyond that, it is pointless to try to defend them on any grounds except taste.

·WHOLEMEAL BREAD·

Making bread does not entail much work but you need to allow time for the yeast to act; you also need a suitable place for the dough to rise. Yeast is a living organism which leavens the bread by giving off carbon dioxide during respiration. When it is activated it starts reproducing: the faster it reproduces, the quicker rising will be. To reproduce, it requires not only food and moisture, which the dough supplies, but a moderate degree of constant warmth. Too low a temperature will mean that the cells reproduce slowly or not at all, as when dough is frozen; sudden cold may kill them. Too high a temperature, as when the dough is finally baked in the oven, also kills them. It helps to avoid draughts during mixing and kneading, and also to warm the bowl used for mixing (but do not allow it to become hot, which will kill the cells which come into contact with it). The dough should be set to rise somewhere warm, such as a bathroom or boiler-room or, in summer, in the sun. If necessary, wrap the bowl in an old towel or blanket.

As the presence of bran means that the yeast cannot feed so directly on wholemeal flour as on white, the time needed for rising is substantially longer. Whereas white flour can be expected to take about 2 hours, wholemeal will probably need 3–4 hours. To this must be added another 30 minutes for re-rising, or 'proving', after the loaf is shaped. This means that you have to allow for an interval of 4–5 hours between mixing the dough and taking the bread from the oven.

The most convenient form of yeast is the dried 'easy-blend' type (available at supermarkets), which is packed in sachets and starts working as soon as the dough is mixed. Fresh yeast must be kept in the refrigerator and used within a short time; it also has to be left for 20 minutes before being added to the flour.

For anyone who prefers fresh yeast, however, directions for using it are given.

As very good bread can be made with frozen dough, I have also appended directions for freezing.

The idea of painting the dough with brine, which helps to give it a crisp crust, comes from *Cranks Breads and Teabreads*, compiled by Daphne Swann.

For 1 large or 2 smaller loaves.

• INGREDIENTS •

*½ oz/15 g fresh yeast and
1 teaspoon soft brown sugar or
1 sachet easy-blend dried yeast*

Fine salt

Warm water

½ oz/15 g full-fat margarine

*Cracked wheat to decorate
(optional)*

*1½ lb/750 g wholemeal flour,
plus extra for kneading*

1 x 2 lb/1 kg or 2 x 1 lb/500 g bread tins

• METHOD •

1 If *using fresh yeast*, stir the yeast and sugar into 3 fl oz/75ml warm water. The water should feel positively warm but not hot. Put in a warm place for 20 minutes or until frothing and creamy. Blend the flour with 1 dessertspoon salt. Rub or stir in the margarine until it has disappeared (there is not enough for it to be evenly distributed throughout the flour, but this will be rectified by kneading). Make a well in the middle and pour in the yeast with 13 fl oz/375 ml more warm water.

2 If *using easy-blend yeast*, blend the flour and salt and rub or stir in the margarine as above. Add and stir in the yeast. Make a well in the middle and pour in ¾ pint/450 ml warm water.

3 Mix to a dough and knead vigorously for at least 5 minutes. At first not all the flour will be taken up, but more will be incorporated as kneading progresses. Treat the dough like dirty washing, pummelling it and pressing it down to the bottom of the bowl. If it seems sticky, add a little extra flour; if much dry flour remains after kneading is finished, tip it out or put the dough into another bowl for rising.

4 Cover with foodwrap and set in a warm place for 3–4 hours or until the dough has doubled in size. If there is nowhere very warm, wrap the bowl in a blanket or towel.

5 Lightly grease the bread tin(s). 'Knock back' the dough by kneading it again for 2–3 minutes. Shape into 1 or 2 ovals and press into the bread tin(s). Cover with foodwrap and return to a warm place to prove for 25–30 minutes or until it has again doubled in size.

6 Pre-heat the oven to 450°F, 230°C, Gas Mark 8. Heat 2 teaspoons salt with 2 tablespoons water until the salt has dissolved. Paint it over the loaf: this produces a crisp crust. Sprinkle with cracked wheat (if using). Make sure that the oven is fully heated. Bake a large loaf for 35 minutes, smaller ones for 30 minutes. Turn out of the tin(s) on to a wire rack to cool.

TO FREEZE THE DOUGH

Put the dough into a covered plastic container or wrap in foodwrap after it has been knocked back. When you wish to bake it, you will have to allow up to 4 hours for defrosting. As the yeast is reactivated it will start to rise: knock it back a second time, shape it, put into a tin and set it to prove in a warm place. Bake as before. The dough may be rather softer than when fresh, but this will not affect the quality of the bread.

• POLENTA •

Describing polenta is difficult: technically, it is baked maize porridge, which does not sound particularly attractive until you stress that it has a crisp top, a melting, creamy texture, especially when made with milk, plus the rich, slightly sweet taste of the maize. You might say that it is the Italian equivalent of Yorkshire pudding or American corn cakes – but it is not at all like either.

Plain polenta is a perfect accompaniment to highly flavoured dishes such as Garlic Mushrooms (see page 84) or Curried Bean Casserole (see page 100); with cheese or cheese and tomatoes on top (in which case it is almost like a version of pizza) you can eat it alone or with plainer dishes such as Cabbage Cheese (see page 166).

It is as cheap, simple and easy to make as possible but, as is usual with very simple dishes, its success depends on small details. By far the most important is that it should be boiled for long enough, because otherwise the meal has a slightly linseedy, raw taste; similarly you need to bake it in a very hot oven. The importance of boiling time was stressed to me by the chef Clara Tomasi, and I mention it particularly because one kind of the meal comes in packets which tell you to boil it for only 4–5 minutes, whereas in fact, for really good polenta, it needs to be simmered for at least 20 minutes.

The taste and texture also depend on whether it is made with milk or water or a proportion of each: with water it will be cakier and less creamy than with milk. Personally I think that the best result is achieved with milk plus a little water – or, although on health grounds I should not recommend this, with skim milk, water and a little cream. (Apart from milk, cream or a cheese top, the only fat it contains is ½ oz/15 g butter.)

The most convenient sort of meal is the so-called 4–5-minute type, which at the moment seems to be available only at good grocers or delicatessens. Ordinary polenta meal, however, can be bought at some supermarkets. Very good, smooth-textured polenta can also be made from the maize flour sold at health-food shops, but I cannot recommend it because, being much more finely ground than the meal, it forms lumps when made into porridge which have to be pressed out, and also sticks to the saucepan.

In fact, in inverse proportion to frequency of stirring, and more so when made with milk, the coarser meal also sticks to the saucepan to some degree: the instant kind is by far the least difficult in this respect. The problem, however, does not affect the quality of the finished polenta and the saucepan will be as clean as new provided that you do not scrape it but leave it to soak.

The porridge can be made in advance – the previous day if you wish (cover and store overnight in the refrigerator). Also, once baked the polenta can be heated up, and may even be better after a second cooking because the top will be crisper and the texture firmer (a cheese top will suffer, though, so if you mean to reheat it, do not add cheese for the first baking). For 4–6.

• INGREDIENTS •

1¾ pints/1 litre milk, skim milk, water or a mixture (I suggest 1¼ pints/750 ml milk plus ½ pint/300 ml water or – less healthy – 1 pint/600 ml skim milk plus 14½ fl oz/430 ml water and 2 tablespoons double cream)

6 oz/190 g polenta meal or (but not recommended) 8 oz/250 g maize flour

½ teaspoon salt

½ oz/15 g butter

TOPPING (OPTIONAL)

4 oz/125 g strong Cheddar or (especially recommended) Gorgonzola cheese or 4 oz/125 g strong Cheddar cheese and 4–5 tomatoes

8½ inch/22 cm tart tin or shallow ovenware dish

• METHOD •

1 Measure the meal into a mug or jug so that you can easily dribble it into the liquid in a slow stream. Bring the milk and/or water to the boil (watch milk carefully to make sure that it does not boil over), then reduce the heat until it is just simmering. Add the salt and butter and pour in the meal slowly and steadily, stirring continuously. Continue stirring for 3–5 minutes or until the porridge has thickened. The 4–5-minute meal will be quite or almost quite smooth. Ordinary meal will form lumps: press them out with the back of the spoon. More will form, but it does not matter: provided that the original ones are broken, the eventual polenta will be smooth. With fine maize flour you will have a serious lump situation: instead of stirring for 3–5 minutes, stir and press for at least 10 minutes.

2 After the initial stirring, simmer 4–5-minute meal for 18–20 minutes, ordinary meal and maize flour for 1 hour, stirring only at intervals. If you can feel that a layer of meal/flour has coated the bottom of the pan, do not try to remove it but leave it to soak off later (you do not want flecks of burnt meal in the finished polenta). Pour the hot porridge into the tart tin or dish.

3 Pre-heat the oven to 450°F, 230°C, Gas Mark 8. If you are adding cheese and/or tomatoes, coarsely grate the cheese and skin and slice the tomatoes, discarding the cores and stalk ends. Arrange the tomatoes and scatter the cheese evenly over the top of the porridge. Bake in the oven for 25 minutes or until beginning to brown. If made with water and without cheese, the polenta will brown only slightly; with milk, more deeply. With Cheddar, it should be golden; with Gorgonzola, which forms a deliciously crisp crust, it will be darker.

To reheat, bake whole or in slices, in the oven at 400-450°F, 200–230°C, Gas Mark 6–8, for about 15 minutes.

• CHEESE SCONES •

These are not only excellent in their own right but, if you have run out of bread, about the quickest possible non-sweet alternative.

As an alternative to butter, spread them with Cheese and

Chilli Dip (see page 18) or cottage cheese with or without chives or dill (see page 19).

• INGREDIENTS •

5 oz/150 g strong Cheddar cheese	Pepper
3 oz/90 g wholemeal flour	2 oz/50 g margarine
6 oz/190 g organic or ordinary white self-raising flour	1 teaspoon mild French mustard (such as Grey Poupon)
Salt	7 tablespoons milk

Baking-sheet

• METHOD •

1 Pre-heat the oven to 400°F, 200°C, Gas Mark 6. Cover the baking-sheet with aluminium foil and grease lightly with butter or oil. Finely grate the cheese.

2 Mix together the flours, ½ teaspoon salt and a generous sprinkling of pepper. Rub or stir in the margarine, then mix in the cheese. Stir the mustard into a little of the milk and add to the mixture with the rest of the milk. Mix, form into balls, set a little apart on the baking-sheet and bake in the oven for 12–15 minutes or until golden-brown.

• AMERICAN MUFFINS •

Among the most memorable breakfasts I have ever had were those at a hotel not in America but in Vancouver, Canada, where they served a salad of strawberries and three different sorts of melon plus a choice of muffins, which were baked to order and arrived still hot from the oven.

American muffins are the equivalent of British scones but much moister. As the mixture is too liquid to hold its shape, they are not moulded or rolled but made in muffin tins or paper cases.

The number of possible kinds of muffin is probably as many

as there are cooks to make them. The banana one below is my approximation of one of those I had at the hotel and the other is designed for convenience, in that you are likely to have the ingredients anyway and can therefore make it on impulse. *Makes 6 bun-sized or 15–16 small cake-sized muffins.*

• BANANA MUFFINS •

• INGREDIENTS •

3½ oz/100 g hazelnuts

2 oz/50 g walnuts or walnut pieces

3½ oz/100 g dark soft brown sugar

3 oz/90 g soft margarine

1 egg (size 2)

1 lemon

3 large bananas

4 oz/125 g wholemeal flour

4 oz/125 g white self-raising flour

1 teaspoon baking-powder

Salt

Bun tins or paper cases

• METHOD •

1 Pre-heat the oven to 350°F, 180°C, Gas Mark 4. Grease the bun tins (if using) with oil. Chop or crush the nuts.

2 Mix together the sugar and margarine and beat in the egg. Wash and dry the lemon and grate the zest into the mixture. Squeeze half of it and add the juice. Mash the bananas and add. Mix together the flours, baking-powder and a pinch of salt and stir in. Spoon into the bun tins or paper cases and bake in the oven for 18–20 minutes or until lightly browned. Eat while still warm.

•MUESLI AND•
HONEY MUFFINS

•INGREDIENTS•

2 oz/50 g walnuts or walnut pieces	5 oz/150 g muesli
3 oz/90 g soft margarine	5 oz/150 g wholemeal flour
2 oz/50 g soft brown sugar	1 teaspoon baking-powder
2 level tablespoons thick honey	1/3 nutmeg
1 egg (size 2)	2 oz/50 g mixed dried fruit
1/4 pint/150 ml milk	2 oz/50 g raisins

Bun tins or paper cases

•METHOD•

1 Pre-heat the oven to 350°F, 180°C, Gas Mark 4. Grease the bun tins (if using) with oil. Roughly crush the nuts.

2 Mix the margarine and sugar. Stir in the honey. Beat in the eggs and stir in the milk. Blend together the muesli, walnuts, flour and baking-powder and grate in the nutmeg. If necessary, separate any fruit which has stuck together and add to the flour. Stir the flour mixture into the milk and honey mixture. Spoon into the bun tins or paper cases and bake in the oven for 15–18 minutes or until a warm golden-brown.

•CHOCOLATE CAKE TO END•
ALL CHOCOLATE CAKES

This is unhealthy and very expensive, but the testing team threatened to go on strike if I did not include it. It is similar to my recipe for Really Extravagant Chocolate Cake in *The Student*

133

Cook Book but even better. Quick and easy to make, its excellence depends largely, as with everything flavoured with chocolate, on the kind of chocolate used. Use plain rather than milk, not too sweet and with a high cocoa content: the higher, the better – and the higher the price. Cooking rather than ordinary chocolate, with its higher fat content, is easier to use, since ordinary chocolate sometimes turns gritty when heated. Easily the best cooking (and eating) chocolate of which I know is Valrhona – but it is nearly twice as expensive as the next best, Menier Chocolat Patissier. Sweeter but a bargain at the price is Sainsbury's Deluxe Chocolate for cooking.

As the cake contains more almonds than flour it will stay fresh and moist for at least a week. So far as finishing it is concerned, this is unlikely to be more than an academic point, but it does mean that you can make it for a particular occasion ahead of time. A tablespoon of brandy instead of coffee or water in which to melt the chocolate also helps it to keep.

You can ice the cake all over or just on top – see below.

• INGREDIENTS •

<table>
<tr><td>6 oz/190 g cooking or plain chocolate</td><td>6 oz/190 g soft brown sugar</td></tr>
<tr><td></td><td>3 eggs (size 2)</td></tr>
<tr><td>1 tablespoon water, brandy or strong made coffee</td><td>2 oz/50 g white or wholemeal self-raising flour</td></tr>
<tr><td>6 oz/190 g soft margarine</td><td>3½ oz/100 g ground almonds</td></tr>
</table>

FILLING

<table>
<tr><td>3 oz/90 g butter</td><td>1½ oz/40 g ground almonds</td></tr>
<tr><td>2 oz/50 g cooking or plain chocolate</td><td></td></tr>
</table>

ICING FOR TOP AND SIDES

<table>
<tr><td>6 oz/190 g cooking or plain chocolate</td><td>1 tablespoon strong made coffee or water</td></tr>
<tr><td>3 oz/90 g butter</td><td>About 2½ oz/70 g icing sugar</td></tr>
</table>

ICING FOR TOP ONLY

4 oz/125 g cooking or
plain chocolate

3 tablespoons strong made coffee
or water

2 oz/50 g butter

About 2½ oz/70 g icing sugar

DECORATION

Almonds or chocolate almonds

8 inch/20 cm loose-bottomed cake tin

• METHOD •

1 Pre-heat the oven to 300°F, 150°F, Gas Mark 2. Line the base of the tin with a circle of greaseproof paper and grease both the paper and the sides of the tin. Melt the chocolate for the cake: break it into squares, put it into a small saucepan with the water, brandy or coffee and set it over very low heat, stirring continuously, until almost melted. Remove from the heat and continue stirring until smooth.

2 Beat the margarine and sugar to a cream. Add and beat in the eggs one by one. When the mixture is smooth, stir in the melted chocolate. Add the flour and ground almonds and mix.

3 The cake can be baked whole but cooks better in two halves. Pour half the mixture into the cake tin and bake in the oven for 30 minutes or until a skewer or knife stuck into the middle comes out clean. Turn upside-down on to a wire rack and leave to cool for 15–20 minutes. Carefully lift off, wash and regrease and reline the tin and bake the second half of the cake as above. (If baked whole, the cake takes 1 hour 10 minutes.)

4 As the filling takes some time to cool and stiffen, make it as soon as the first half of the cake is in the oven. Chop the butter into small pieces and break up the chocolate. Put into a small saucepan over very low heat and stir until the chocolate is nearly liquified, then remove from the heat and continue stirring until smooth. Add and stir in the ground almonds. If the filling is not stiff enough to spread by the time both halves of the cake are cold, chill in the refrigerator.

5 Make the icing. Break up the chocolate and chop the butter.

Put into a small saucepan with the coffee or water and melt as above. Stir in the icing sugar. The mixture should be as firm as dough: if it too liquid to hold its shape, it will run off the cake. If necessary, add a little more icing sugar. Fill a mug with very hot water and spread the icing over the cake using a table knife constantly dipped in it (this prevents the icing from sticking to the blade). Smooth the surface with the hot, wet knife and decorate.

• EGGLESS FRUIT CAKE •

That this cake is suitable for vegans is by no means its only recommendation: it is also, in my view, even richer-tasting than the equivalent made in the usual way with eggs. It is, however, slightly softer-textured and more crumbly, so that you need to take it out of the tin carefully and cut it with a sharp knife.

As with other fruit cakes, the fruit and nuts can be varied. Apricots with almonds and orange zest give a tangy, refreshing taste, whereas apple juice with currants, lemon zest and pecans produce a flavour almost like that of good mincemeat. With these ingredients, especially, it is very suitable for a Christmas or birthday cake: I have therefore included recipes for Eggless Almond Paste and Icing. The addition of a little brandy not only enhances the flavour but also ensures that the cake will keep; even without it, however, an iced cake will stay fresh for at least a week in an airtight container.

Allow 1¼–1½ hours for the All-Bran to soak.

• INGREDIENTS •

3 oz/90 g All-Bran

½ pint/300 ml soya milk, apple juice or milk

8 oz/250 g soft margarine or butter

3½ oz/100 g almonds, pecans or hazelnuts

3½ oz/100 g walnut pieces

8oz/125 g mixed dried fruit

8 oz/250 g dark soft brown sugar

1 tablespoon brandy (optional)

6 oz/190 g plain wholemeal or white flour

4 oz/125 g no-soak dried apricots,   *1 orange or lemon*
   currants or raisins

**8 inch/20 cm loose-bottomed cake tin
about 3¼ inches/8 cm deep**

• METHOD •

1 Leave the All-Bran to soak in the soya milk, apple juice or milk for 1¼–1½ hours. If you are using butter, take it out of the refrigerator and chop it into small pieces so that it softens (this makes mixing easier).

2 Roughly chop or crush the nuts (a few sizeable pieces add interest to the cake). Chop the apricots (if using) into small pieces; pick over the other dried fruit to ensure that it is not stuck together.

3 Pre-heat the oven to 300°F, 150°C, Gas Mark 2. Line the bottom of the cake tin with a circle of aluminium foil and generously grease the foil and the sides of the tin. Beat together the fat and sugar. Stir in the soaked All-Brain, nuts, dried fruit and brandy (if you are using it). Wash and dry the orange or lemon and finely grate the zest into the mixture. Stir in the flour. Turn into the cake tin and bake in the oven for 30 minutes. Turn down the oven to 250°F, 120°C, Gas Mark ½, and bake for a further 30–40 minutes or until a skewer or knife stuck into the centre of the cake comes out clean. Remove from the oven and leave in the tin to cool. Turn upside-down to remove the sides and bottom of the tin in the usual way (run a knife round the sides of the cake to loosen). Slide on to an upturned plate.

• EGGLESS ALMOND PASTE •

The ready-made almond paste sold in grocers' shops and supermarkets is flavoured with almond essence; this version is flavoured with lemon and tastes quite different – much sharper and less cloying on the palate. A whole lemon gives a fairly pronounced flavour, which I personally like, but if you prefer you can use the juice of only half and add an extra tablespoon of water to make up the quantity.

The quantities given below will produce enough paste for a fairly thin layer all over the cake. For a thicker layer you will need 2–3 oz/50–90 g more almonds and icing sugar, plus a little extra water.

The usual way of sticking the paste to the cake is with apricot jam, but any kind of jam will do provided that the flavour is not too obvious or unsympathetic to that of the cake. Good alternatives are plum or marmalade; the worst I can think of is blackcurrant.

Allow a couple of hours for the paste to dry out before adding the top icing (if you like, leave it overnight).

• INGREDIENTS •

7 oz/200 g ground almonds	Juice 1 smallish lemon
8 oz/250 g icing sugar	1 tablespoon apricot or other jam or marmalade

• METHOD •

1 Mix together the ground almonds and sugar. Squeeze the lemon juice and add with 1 dessertspoon water. Gradually add as much more water as is needed to form a firm dough: exactly how much will depend on the juiciness of the lemon, but it will probably take most of another dessertspoonful. It is important that the dough should not be too soft or it will be difficult to mould.

2 Put the jam or marmalade with a few drops of lemon juice into a small saucepan and melt over low heat. When liquid, paint or spread very thinly over the top and sides of the cake, avoiding or removing any bits of fruit or peel (strictly speaking, the jam should be strained, but for such a small quantity this is hardly worthwhile).

3 Bought almond paste can be rolled out like pastry, but rolling is impracticable with this recipe: moulding the dough and smoothing the surface with a knife will give almost if not quite as good a result. Shape the dough into a flattish disc, place on the cake and gently mould it over the top and down the sides. Use the flat side of a blunt knife dipped in hot water to level and smooth it. Make a slight rim round the edge of the cake: this makes it easier to square off the icing. Leave to dry.

•ICING•

I am giving instructions only for the basic coating: I leave decoration to you. If you want to try piping, make some extra icing and cut a small hole in the corner of a plastic foodbag to use as a nozzle. Unless you have done it before, I suggest practising on something other than the cake, or stick to nuts or chocolates as cake decorations (which taste better anyhow).

•INGREDIENTS•

Juice 1 lemon

Decorations

1 lb/500 g icing sugar

•METHOD•

1 Squeeze the lemon and add the juice with 1 dessertspoon cold water to the sugar. As with the almond paste, you will need more water: add enough by degrees to make a firm lump (it will probably take just over 2 teaspoons). If it ends up too soft to hold its shape, you will have to add more icing sugar.

2 Have ready a mug of very hot water and a round-bladed knife. Place the icing on the almond paste and spread into a smooth layer over the top and sides with the blade of the knife dipped into the hot water (you will need to keep dipping). Make a tidy rim at the edges. Decorate. The icing will take about 24 hours to dry.

• PEAR AND ALMOND TART •

One of the cheapest kinds of fruit you can buy is the long brown or speckled Conference pear, which does not have as much flavour as some other varieties (notably Williams) but is excellent for cooking: in particular it is useful in winter when the choice of fresh cooking fruit is limited.

At the right stage of ripeness pears give a little to the touch: avoid any which are definitely soft, as they will be overripe. If they are hard and underripe, you can still use them, but they will take a relatively long time to stew (in fact, you may prefer them slightly unripe, as they are crisper and less sweet).

The tart can be eaten hot or cold. Serve with Greek yoghurt or Yoghurt Cheese (see page 180) instead of cream. For 6–8.

• INGREDIENTS •

1 quantity Shortcrust Pastry with Wholemeal and White Flour (see page 53)

1 lb/500 g Conference pears

8 oz/250 g caster sugar, plus a little extra for sprinkling

2 oz/50 g butter

3½ oz/100 g ground almonds

Juice ½ lemon

1 generous dessertspoon plum jam, apple jelly or marmalade

½ inch/1 cm piece cinnamon stick

8½ inch/22 cm tart tin
Fish-slice or slotted spoon

• METHOD •

1 Pre-heat the oven to 400°F, 200°C, Gas Mark 6. Line the tart tin with the pastry. Cover all over, including the rim, with aluminium foil, pressing it closely to the edges. Bake in the oven for 10 minutes. Remove the foil and bake for a further 5 minutes. Take the pastry case out of the oven and turn down the heat to 350°F, 180°C, Gas Mark 4.

2 Quarter, peel, core and slice the pears. Put with 4 oz/125 g of

the sugar (no water) in a pan over very low heat for about 2 minutes or until the sugar has melted and the juice has started to run; turn frequently. Raise the heat slightly and poach for 5 minutes or until the fruit is tender and submerged, or almost submerged, in liquid. Lift out the pieces with the fish-slice or slotted spoon, leaving the juice in the pan.

3 Melt the butter over gentle heat (do not allow it to brown). Remove from the heat. Mix with the remaining 4 oz/125 g sugar. Add the ground almonds and just enough lemon juice for the mixture to become a stiff paste.

4 Spread the jam, jelly or marmalade evenly over the half-cooked pastry case. Cover with an even layer of the almond mixture. Arrange the slices of pear in a circle over the paste, fat ends outwards; pile any left-over pieces in a knob in the middle.

5 Pound the cinnamon stick as finely as you can. Set the pan of pear juice over high heat and boil for 1¼–1½ minutes or until slightly thickened and reduced to a syrup. Pour this over the pears. Sprinkle with the cinnamon and a little more sugar and bake in the oven for 35 minutes.

• PECAN PIE •

Both pecans and the maple syrup, with which the filling is made, are expensive, but everyone agrees that the cost is worth it. You could use only 4 oz/125 g nuts rather than 5 oz/150 g if you prefer, and I have been as economical as possible with the syrup. It is important, however, that the syrup should be pure: you can buy cheaper, part-maple syrup (probably labelled 'pancake syrup'), but it will not give the pie at all the same flavour.

To contrast with the texture of the roughly chopped nuts, the filling does not set hard but is soft and creamy. When just baked, it will be slightly puffed up and cracked but will subside as the pie cools.

It should be a deep, rich brown: do not think that it is burnt because of its dark colour (which is due to the darkness of the sugar and syrup). For 4–5.

• INGREDIENTS •

3 oz/90 g butter

5 oz/150 g pecan nuts

1 quantity Shortcrust Pastry with Wholemeal Flour (see page 52) or Shortcrust Pastry with Wholemeal and White Flour (see page 53)

6 oz/190 g dark soft brown sugar

2 eggs (size 2)

1 teaspoon cornflour

4 fl oz/125 ml maple syrup

8½ inch/22 cm tart tin

• METHOD •

1 Pre-heat the oven to 400°F, 200°C, Gas Mark 6. Take the butter out of the refrigerator, chop it into small pieces and leave it in a warm place to soften. Roughly chop or crush the nuts, leaving some almost whole.

2 Line the tart tin with the pastry. Cover all over, including the rim, with aluminium foil, pressing it closely to the edges of the tin. Bake in the oven for 10 minutes, then remove the foil and bake for another 5 minutes. Take the pastry case out of the oven and lower the temperature to 350°F, 180°C, Gas Mark 4.

3 Beat the butter with the sugar to a thick paste. Add and beat in the eggs one at a time. Stir in the cornflour.

4 Add the nuts and syrup. Stir vigorously, pour at once into the pastry case (if you leave the mixture to stand for any length of time, it will need stirring again, because the syrup sinks to the bottom). Bake in the oven for 15 minutes. Turn the oven down to 300°F, 150°C, Gas Mark 2, and cook for a further 15–20 minutes or until set (tilt the dish slightly: if the filling moves, it is not ready). Leave to cool before serving.

·PARTIES AND·
DINNER-PARTIES

If you are expecting a large, perhaps indefinite number of people at uncertain times, you need dishes which can either be kept hot or eaten cold, and preferably of the kind which will stretch. Start with as many Walnut and Blue Cheese Straws as you have the patience to make; dips, such as Guacamole (page 15) or Clara's Lentil and Lime Pâté (page 16), are always a good idea – though if you think guests may eat them with the straws, choose Cheese and Chilli Dip (page 18). For hot dishes I suggest Pepper and Nut Pilaf (page 68) or lasagne or Louise's Vegetable Kebabs in this chapter: the kebabs have the advantage that they can be grilled in relays as required. With any of these serve green salad – parties being the one occasion when it may be worth buying several kinds of lettuce or other salad greens: for instance, batavia or Cos lettuce with radiccio and chicory or oakleaf with lamb's lettuce and perhaps diced red pepper.

As a sweet you could serve Chocolate Cake to End All Chocholate Cakes (page 133), which is light but very rich so that people will not need much; or you could choose Pecan Pie (page 141), Pear and Almond Tart (page 140) or Yoghurt Ices (page 178), which can be made well in advance. Three more suggestions, all made with fruit, are given in this chapter, of which the cheapest will probably be Spiced Apple Yoghurt with Gin. If you choose Summer Pudding, you will need to make at least two, which will call for 2¾ lb/1.25 kg soft fruit (it may be a good idea to go to a pick-your-own fruit farm, where, even if the fruit is not especially cheap, it will be absolutely fresh and you can ensure that it is in good condition).

For a dinner-party you can again serve dips, with plates of colourful crudités, or perhaps small portions of salads such as Tuscan-style Bean and Tomato (page 118), Tomato and Mozarella (page 116) or Avocado and Almond (page 122). As contrast is important, however, do not serve a salad containing cheese if the next course also includes it.

The main course could be Cannelloni (page 47) or Mushroom Risotto (page 66), both with a plain green salad; or you could serve Curried Egg and Mushroom Pie (page 57), perhaps with broccoli, Clara's Spiced Lentils with Stewed Mushrooms (pages 97 and 86), or one of the three slightly more elaborate dishes given in this chapter.

I selected the three sweets in this chapter because they are relatively healthy – fruit salad completely so and Summer Pudding containing only fruit, bread and a relatively small amount of sugar. It could be accompanied by Yoghurt Cheese (page 180) instead of cream; fruit salad needs neither.

If you wish to serve coffee afterwards, buy it freshly roasted and ground if you possibly can, since, like spices (and despite air-tight packaging), if it is ready-ground it will have lost much of its flavour.

A coffee-pot is unnecessary: you can make first-class coffee in a jug, using a tea-strainer as you pour it out. For those who like it white, heat but do not boil milk; serve with Demerara or soft brown sugar.

• WALNUT AND •
BLUE CHEESE STRAWS

Whereas the point of ordinary cheese straws is their lightness (hence their name), these are crisp and crunchy. If made with white flour, they are also very light; if with a proportion of brown flour, slightly more solid but crunchier.

I have tried turning them into more decorative twists, but do not recommend it. For tidy twists, you need to make the pastry in a slightly different way which produces a less crisp result: I have given precedence to eating quality. *Makes 40–50.*

• INGREDIENTS •

3½ oz/100 g walnut pieces	Pepper
6 oz/190 g Danish Blue cheese	Salt

*6 oz/190 g white self-raising flour
or 4 oz/125 g white self-raising flour
and 2 oz/50 g granary flour,
plus extra for dusting*

*3 oz/90 g butter straight from
the refrigerator*

**Rolling-pin (or clean milk or beer bottle)
Board or surface for rolling out
Baking-sheet**

• METHOD •

1 Crush the nuts fairly finely. Finely grate the cheese.

2 Mix together the flours if necessary, then add and blend in a sprinkling of pepper and ¾ teaspoon salt (unless you are using heavily salted butter, in which case reduce the salt to ½ teaspoon). Mix with the nuts and cheese.

3 Dust a rolling-pin and rolling-out surface with flour. Chop the cold butter into 8 thin slices. Make a well in the flour mixture and measure into it 4 tablespoons very cold water. Turn with a spoon to mix, then wash your hands and form it into dough by hand. Roll it out into an oblong. Put 2 slices of butter on top, sprinkle with a little white flour and fold in half. Repeat the rolling and folding three times. Leave to rest for 15–20 minutes in the refrigerator.

4 Pre-heat the oven to 400°F, 200°C, Gas Mark 6. Line the baking-sheet with aluminium foil and grease very lightly with margarine. Roll the dough into an oblong slightly less than ¼ inch/5 mm thick (but no thinner). Cut into fingers about ½ inch/1 cm wide and 2½–2¾ inches/6–7 cm long. Gather up the trimmings, re-roll them and cut more straws. Repeat, keeping the rolling-pin and surface dusted with flour, until all the dough is used. Bake for 8–10 minutes or until lightly browned.

• FILO PASTRY •
SPINACH ROLLS

Filo pastry is kneaded and rolled into sheets almost as thin as tissue-paper, which can be spread with a filling, as for strudel or baclava, or used as a wrapping for a solid stuffing, as here. It is normally bought rather than made domestically and has to be sold frozen because the sheets dry out and become brittle very quickly. It is easy to handle except that it does have a tendency to tear.

I have given two fillings, the first with cinnamon and raisins and the second, which is similar to the one for Cannelloni (page 47), flavoured with cheese. The quantities for each fill 6 medium-sized rolls, for which you will need 4 oz/125 g pastry: as the pastry is often sold in 8 oz/270 g packets, you will either have to make both or a double amount of one to finish it. Allow it 1½ hours at room temperature or 3–4 hours in the refrigerator to defrost. Do not unwrap it until you are ready to use it.

Frozen (preferably leaf) spinach can be used for the cheese stuffing but real fresh spinach is essential for the cinnamon one.

The spinach-and-cinnamon-filled rolls should be served with Red Pepper Sauce (see page 149); as the sauce needs to simmer for 20–25 minutes, prepare it before you stuff the rolls so that it cooks while the pastry bakes. The cheese-filled rolls go well with cauliflower in a light cheese sauce or with Alex's Normandy Potatoes made without Cheddar cheese (page 171).

• SPINACH AND CINNAMON FILLING •

It makes all the difference in this recipe to use freshly crushed rather than ready-ground cinnamon. *Fills 6 filo pastry rolls.*

• INGREDIENTS •

1 *lb/500 g spinach*	*⅔ inch/1.5 cm piece cinnamon stick*
Salt	1 *tablespoon oil*
1 *medium onion*	1 *oz/25 g pine nuts*
½ *large red pepper*	1 *oz/25 g raisins*
2 *teaspoons coriander seeds*	6 *oz/190 g medium-fat soft cheese*

Large saucepan with a lid

• METHOD •

1 Pick over the spinach, discarding any weeds or damaged leaves, and wash, twice if necessary. Put into the large saucepan with ½ teaspoon salt and 1 tablespoon water, cover and set over medium to high heat for 4 minutes. Stir, then cook for 1–2 minutes more or until the spinach is submerged in juice and tender. Drain and press out surplus liquid with the back of a spoon. Chop roughly.

2 Peel and finely chop the onion. Wash and dry the pepper, remove the seeds, the white inner membrane and any dark spots and dice the flesh finely. Crush the coriander and cinnamon.

3 Fry the onion and pepper in the oil over low heat, turning often, for about 12 minutes or until soft. Add the spices and nuts and fry for 2–3 minutes. Stir in the raisins. Remove from the heat and stir in the spinach. Turn the cheese into a bowl and soften with a fork. Add the spinach to it and mix.

• CHEESE AND SPINACH FILLING •

Fills 6 filo pastry rolls.

• INGREDIENTS •

1 lb/500 g spinach	1 tablespoon oil
Salt	1 oz/25 g pine nuts
½ large red pepper	4 oz/125 g ricotta or other
4–5 cloves garlic	fresh-tasting medium-fat soft cheese
3 oz/90 g Parmesan cheese	

Large saucepan with a lid

• METHOD •

1 Wash, cook, drain and chop the spinach as for Spinach and Cinnamon Filling.

2 Prepare the red pepper as for Spinach and Cinnamon Filling. Peel and finely chop the garlic. Grate the Parmesan. Fry the pepper in the oil over moderate heat, turning frequently, for 4–5 minutes or until just showing signs of changing colour. Add the garlic and fry for another 1–2 minutes or until the garlic is pale gold and the pepper darkening. Add the nuts, turn quickly in the oil and remove from the heat. Stir in the spinach. Add and stir in the Parmesan. Turn the soft cheese into a bowl and loosen with a fork if necessary. Add the spinach mixture to it. and combine thoroughly.

• MAKING THE ROLLS •

Makes 6 rolls.

• INGREDIENTS •

4 oz/125 g frozen filo pastry, thawed   *Prepared filling*

*1 oz/25 g butter or about
2 tablespoons oil*

**Pastry-brush
Surface for spreading the pastry
Baking-sheet**

• METHOD •

1 Pre-heat the oven to 400°F, 200°C, Gas Mark 6. If you are using butter, melt it: chop it into pieces and put in a small saucepan over very low heat until it is almost liquified, then remove from the heat and stir until completely liquid (it is important not to let it brown). Line the baking-sheet with aluminium foil and paint thinly with a little of the melted butter or with oil.

2 Unwrap the pastry and lay a sheet on the surface. Cut into pieces 12 inches/30 cm long and 8–10 inches/20–25 cm wide. Paint with butter or oil. Fold each in half along the longer side to make a smaller oblong. Place 1 generous tablespoon of the filling along one short edge, leaving a margin of about 1 inch/2.5 cm. Fold over about ½ inch/1 cm of each long edge neatly towards the middle. Roll up the pastry, starting from the short edge nearest the filling, and place on the baking-sheet. Repeat until the pastry and filling are used, setting the rolls a little apart. Brush each with butter or oil and bake in the oven for 15–20 minutes or until crisp and golden.

•RED PEPPER SAUCE•

This recipe makes quite a lot: if there is any left over, eat it with Yoghurt Cheese (page 180) on a Baked Potato (page 167) or with pasta.

•INGREDIENTS•

1 lb/500 g ripe tomatoes	1 tablespoon oil
1 large red pepper	Salt
1 onion	Pepper
3 cloves garlic	1 teaspoon soft brown sugar
2 teaspoons coriander seeds	1½ tablespoons tomato purée
1 red chilli	

•METHOD•

1 Peel and chop the tomatoes. Wash, dry and quarter the pepper, discarding the core; pick out all the seeds, trim off the white inner membrane and any dark spots and dice the flesh finely. Peel and finely chop the onion and garlic. Crush the coriander. Wash, dry and trim the stalk end from the chilli; discard the seeds and dice as finely as possible. Do not rub your eyes while handling it and wash your hands directly afterwards (or wear polythene gloves).

2 Fry the onion and pepper in the oil over low heat, turning frequently, for 12 minutes or until soft. Add the garlic and fry for 3–4 minutes. Add the coriander and fry for 1–2 minutes. Add the tomatoes, season lightly with salt and moderately with pepper, and simmer for 7–10 minutes, pressing the flesh against the bottom of the pan until liquified. Stir in the sugar and tomato purée and simmer for a further 20–25 minutes until the sauce has reduced to the consistency you require.

• CHICK PEA AND •
YOGHURT LASAGNE

The pasta in this dish is layered with yoghurt rather than with the more conventional cheese sauce not for health reasons but because it gives a sharper, more interesting flavour.

As dried pasta for lasagne which does not need boiling before use is now usual, I have assumed that this is the sort you will use. If, however, yours does require pre-cooking, follow the instructions on the packet and do not start boiling it until the filling is ready, because if it is allowed to become cold before use, the sheets will stick together. The amount you need varies slightly according to the thickness of the pasta and the size of your dish. If the sheets are relatively thick, as freshly made ones often are, or the dish is wider than the size specified, buy a little extra.

The aubergines are grilled because they are very absorbent and if fried will soak up a considerable quantity of oil, which is not only fattening but (as it really should be olive) expensive too. Allow 30 minutes–1 hour for them to sweat. The filling (but not the cheese sauce) can be prepared in advance. *For 5–6.*

• INGREDIENTS •

4 oz/125 g chick peas, soaked
overnight in cold water

Salt, some of which should be
finely ground

2 largish aubergines

2 lb/1 kg ripe tomatoes

1 red pepper

1 green pepper

Small bunch parsley (enough for
2 tablespoons when chopped)

2 teaspoons coriander seeds

2 dried chillies

About 4–6 tablespoons
olive oil

Pepper

1 teaspoon soft brown sugar

3 tablespoons tomato purée

2–2½ oz/50–70 g Parmesan cheese

3 scant teaspoons cornflour

1 *medium–large onion*

4 *cloves garlic*

14 *oz/440 g Greek or other mild, creamy yoghurt*

12–14 *oz/375–440 g lasagne*

CHEESE SAUCE

¾ *pint/450 ml milk*

1 *bayleaf*

2 *oz/50 g Parmesan cheese*

¾ *oz/20 g butter or 1½ tablespoons oil*

¾ *oz/20 g flour*

Salt

Pepper

Small saucepan with a lid
Large baking-sheet
Ovenware dish about 12 inches/30 cm long,
8½ inches/22 cm wide and 2½ inches/6 cm deep

• METHOD •

1 Drain the chick peas, rinse and put into the saucepan with a lid. Add quite a lot of fresh cold water (but no salt). Bring to the boil, skim and boil fast for 10 minutes. Lower the heat, cover and simmer for 1¼ hours, adding more water if necessary. Add a little salt and continue to simmer for 15–30 minutes or until tender. Drain.

2 Wash the aubergines, trim the ends and cut into slices ¼ inch/5 mm thick. Sprinkle with fine salt and put into a sieve or colander to sweat for 30 minutes–1 hour. Rinse thoroughly under the cold tap and leave to drain.

3 Peel and chop the tomatoes. Wash, dry and quarter the peppers, discard the cores, seeds and white inner membrane, cut out any dark spots on the red one and slice the flesh into fairly narrow strips. Trim the parsley stems; wash, blot dry and chop finely. Peel and finely chop the onion and garlic. Crush the coriander seeds. Wash, dry and trim the stalk ends of the chillies; pick out all the seeds and dice the flesh as finely as possible.

4 Fry the onions and peppers in 2 tablespoons of the oil over low heat, stirring frequently, for 12–15 minutes or until soft. Add the garlic and fry for 3–4 minutes. Add the chillies and turn in the oil. Add the coriander and fry for 1–2 minutes. Add the tomatoes, season lightly with salt and fairly generously with pepper and simmer for 7–10 minutes, pressing the flesh against the bottom of the pan until liquified. Stir in the sugar and tomato purée and simmer for 15–20 minutes. Add the chick peas and parsley, then remove from the heat. If making the filling in advance, allow to cool, cover and store in the refrigerator.

5 Pre-heat the grill to medium heat. Line 2 plates with kitchen paper and the baking-sheet with aluminium foil. Blot the aubergine slices dry if necessary. Either paint each side with oil and set as many as will fit on the baking-sheet (you may have to grill them in 2 sessions) or spread 2 tablespoons oil over the sheet and turn the slices as you place them on it so that both sides are coated with oil. If the oil is absorbed before all the slices are moistened, add a little more (if the slices have to be grilled in 2 sessions, you may need another 2 tablespoons). Season very lightly with salt and grill for 5–7 minutes or until light brown, or mottled with brown, on each side – the slices will not colour evenly, tending to brown fastest in the middle. Transfer to the paper-lined plates.

6 Grate the Parmesan. Mix the cornflour with the yoghurt. Spread a third each of the vegetable filling, aubergine, yoghurt and pasta, in that order, in the bottom of the dish, sprinkling the yoghurt with Parmesan. Repeat twice to make 3 layers.

7 Make the cheese sauce for the top. Heat but do not boil the milk with the bayleaf, remove from the heat and leave for a few minutes to infuse. Grate the Parmesan. Pre-heat the oven to 400°F, 200°C, Gas Mark 6. Melt the butter or warm the oil over low heat. Stir in the flour. As soon as it is absorbed, pour in the milk slowly, stirring continuously. Keep stirring until the sauce is thick. Season lightly with salt and fairly generously with pepper and simmer for 5–6 minutes. Remove from the heat and stir in the cheese. Pour over the lasagne, taking care to cover all the pasta (if it is not covered, it will become brown and brittle) and bake in the oven for 25–30 minutes or until the top is golden and bubbling.

•POLLY'S CHESTNUT TARTS• WITH HAZELNUT PASTRY

For a dinner-party individual tarts, made in muffin tins, look very festive, but you can, if you prefer, cook one large tart instead. Use pastry made with half white flour – all wholemeal cloaks the taste and texture of the hazelnuts. Large mushrooms usually have more flavour but button ones will give a crisper texture to the finished dish; either are suitable.

If possible, time the tarts so that you are ready to eat them as soon as the pastry and filling are cooked. They can be heated for 5–10 minutes in the oven but the pastry will be crisper and they will look more attractive if they are served straight away. Accompany with wedges of lemon and plain boiled green beans, broccoli or cauliflower: arrange the vegetables in a circle around individual tarts. *For 6.*

• INGREDIENTS •

4 oz/125 g dried chestnuts, soaked overnight in cold water	½ oz/15 g butter
Salt	1 tablespoon groundnut or sunflower oil
3 sticks celery	Pepper
About ¼ pint/150 ml milk	½ oz/15 g white flour
8 oz/250 g mushrooms	1 teaspoon cornflour
1 medium onion	4 teaspoons lemon juice
4 cloves garlic	1½ tablespoons dark soy sauce
About ¾ inch/2 cm piece fresh root ginger	Lemon wedges to serve

PASTRY

2½ oz/70 g hazelnuts	4 oz/125 g butter
4 oz/125 g plain white flour	About 2 tablespoons cold water

4 oz/125 g wholemeal flour   *1 dessertspoon oil*

Muffin tins or 8½ inch/20 cm tart tin

• METHOD •

1 Drain, rinse and pick over the soaked chestnuts, removing any black patches and pieces of dark skin. Cover with cold water, bring to the boil and simmer for 40 minutes. Add a generous pinch of salt and simmer for 10 minutes more or until tender when prodded with a fork. Drain and chop roughly.

2 Make the pastry. Crush the nuts finely, mix with the flours and proceed as for Shortcrust Pastry with Wholemeal and White Flour (see page 53). Use the pastry to line the tin(s). For muffin tins cut the pastry with a saucer if you have one the right size; otherwise cut circles with a knife. Cover with aluminium foil, moulded into the indentation(s).

3 Trim the leaf and root ends of the celery, peel off any brownish streaks, wash and slice finely. Just cover with salted water, bring to the boil and boil gently for 10 minutes or until tender but still crisp. Drain over a bowl; keep the cooking liquor and make up to ½ pint/300 ml with the milk.

4 Trim the mushroom stalks. Peel and rinse large mushrooms; wash button ones. Blot dry with kitchen paper and chop or slice finely. Peel and finely chop the onion and garlic. Peel and dice the ginger, discarding any fibrous patches.

5 Pre-heat the oven to 400°F, 200°C, Gas Mark 6. Put the pastry into the oven when you start frying the mushrooms (see below). Bake for 10 minutes. Remove the foil and bake for 15 minutes more or until golden.

6 Melt the butter in the oil and fry the onion for 8–10 minutes, turning often, until soft but not brown. Add the garlic and ginger and fry for 3–4 minutes. Add the mushrooms, season lightly with salt and more generously with pepper and fry for 5–7 minutes or until soft; they will soak up the fat for the first few minutes, so add a little more butter if necessary. Add the flour and stir until amalgamated. Pour in the celery liquor and milk and stir continuously until thickened. Add the celery and chestnuts and simmer, stirring frequently, for 10–15 minutes or until the pastry is baked. Stir in the cornflour, lemon juice and soy sauce. Spoon the filling into the pastry case(s) and serve.

• LOUISE'S VEGETABLE •
KEBABS
WITH SATAY SAUCE

These are a brilliant idea for parties of any sort. For a buffet meal you can grill them on small skewers in relays, or for a dinner-party on long ones all at once. They take only 10–12 minutes to cook, most of the work has to be done in advance, which leaves plenty of time for other preparations, and the kebabs look festive and colourful, particularly if you succeed in finding a yellow courgette. The cost is also very reasonable, the only relatively expensive item (apart from peanut butter for the sauce) being cherry tomatoes – but you do not need many. The recipe is long because of the sauce and marinade: in fact, however, it is easy and, in terms of working time, quick.

I have not suggested cherry tomatoes elsewhere in this book because they really are rather expensive. They are tiny, as the name implies, and at present the only sort which are fairly certain to have flavour. Here they are needed both for flavour and size; most large supermarkets sell them, but if you cannot obtain any, use the smallest ordinary ones you can find. A yellow courgette (which is simply a variety of the green) looks attractive but is not essential. Try to match the diameter of the mushroom caps with the width of the courgettes.

Set the vegetables to marinate about 8 hours before you wish to grill them. The sauce can also be prepared in advance: if convenient, make it at the same time as the marinade. Allow 30 minutes–1 hour for the courgettes to sweat.

Serve with rice and thick yoghurt. *Enough for 10–12 long skewers or about 30 short ones.*

• INGREDIENTS •

1 lb/500 g courgettes (3 or 4 including 1 yellow one)	1 large green pepper
	3 medium onions
Salt	8 oz/250 g cherry tomatoes

155

12 oz/375 g button mushrooms

1 large red pepper

Pepper

Groundnut oil

MARINADE

1 lemon

1 teaspoon honey

2 tablespoons groundnut oil

2 tablespoons dark soy sauce

2 tablespoons wine vinegar

3 tablespoons soft brown sugar

1 teaspoon paprika

1 teaspoon chilli powder

Pepper

SATAY SAUCE

1 medium onion

6 cloves garlic

2 dried chillies

2 tablespoons groundnut oil

12 oz/375 g smooth peanut butter

¼ pint/150 ml milk

2 limes

1 small lemon

2 tablespoons dark soy sauce

1 teaspoon paprika

2 tablespoons soft brown sugar

Pepper

TO SERVE

Rice (see page 60)

1 lb/500 g Greek or other thick mild yoghurt

**Thick saucepan
Grill-pan
10–12 long metal skewers or 30 short wooden ones**

• METHOD •

1 Trim the ends of the courgettes and pare off any damaged or discoloured pieces of skin. Wash and cut into ¼ inch/5 mm or even thinner slices. Sprinkle with fine salt and leave to drain in a sieve or colander for 30 minutes–1 hour. Rinse under the cold tap and leave to dry on kitchen paper.

2 Make the marinade. Squeeze the lemon. Put the honey into a cup and beat in the lemon juice. Place all the other ingredients for the marinade, including a generous sprinkling of pepper, into a large bowl. Add the honey and lemon, then make up to ¾ pint/450 ml with water.

3 Trim the mushroom stalks, wash the mushrooms, blot dry with kitchen paper and put into the marinade. Wash and quarter the peppers, removing the cores and all the seeds; trim off the white inner membranes, cut out any dark spots on the red one and chop the flesh into pieces about the same size as or a little bigger than the mushrooms. Add to the marinade. Peel the onions and cut into fine slices; add. Add the courgettes. Stir the vegetables in the liquid: there should be nearly enough to cover all of them. (I have not suggested adding the tomatoes because they are not absorbent and will take up space.) Put a large plate over the bowl and leave in a cool place for 8 hours. Stir from time to time, taking care to immerse any vegetables at the top not covered by the marinade.

4 Make the sauce. Peel and very finely chop the onion and garlic. Wash, dry and trim the stalk ends of the chillies; slit, remove all the seeds and dice the flesh as finely as possible. Do not rub your eyes while handling them and wash your hands directly afterwards (or wear polythene gloves). Fry the onions in the oil over low heat for 5 minutes or until beginning to soften. Add the garlic and fry for 4–5 minutes. Add the chillies and fry for 3–4 minutes or until the onions and garlic are soft but not brown. Allow to cool. Add the peanut butter, milk and 3 fl oz/75 ml water and stir until homogenous. Squeeze the limes and lemon and stir the juice into the sauce. Add and stir in the soy, paprika, sugar and a generous sprinkling of pepper. Cover and leave in the refrigerator or a cool place.

5 Set the rice to cook 30 minutes before you wish to serve. Put the sauce to warm over very low heat, preferably in a thick saucepan, while the kebabs grill; stir frequently. If the sauce seems very thick, add a little more water.

6 Hull and wash the tomatoes. Line the grill-pan with aluminium foil. Pre-heat the grill to medium heat if you have a choice. Thread the vegetables on to the skewers, alternating the different kinds. Incomplete slices of onion may fall off; cook them in the pan under the kebabs. (The onion slices will be bigger than the other vegetables, but this does not matter.) Do not pack the vegetables very closely or they will not cook properly. Lay the skewers across the pan at a little distance apart. Sprinkle each with pepper and drizzle with groundnut oil. Grill at medium heat (or about 6 inches/15 cm from the element under a hot grill) for 5 minutes, basting at least twice. Turn and grill for 5–7 more minutes or until the courgettes and onions are just starting to brown. Set on a bed of rice, moistened with the juices from the bottom of the pan, and serve the sauce and yoghurt separately.

•Summer Pudding•

One of the attractions of this is that it is moulded in a pudding basin and looks like a traditional pudding – yet it consists only of soft fruit, bread and relatively little sugar (no fat). It is very easy to make, since it involves no cooking except sweating some of the fruit to make the juices run. The only point to note is that it needs to be weighted, which means either that the basin must be full enough for a plate on the top to squeeze it down or that a smaller plate or saucer must fit closely inside.

The pudding has to be made a day ahead. Use stale bread; it will absorb the fruit juices more readily. *For 6–8.*

•INGREDIENTS•

8 oz/250 g bilberries, gooseberries, blackberries or red currants

4 oz/125 g caster sugar

8 oz/250 g raspberries

6 oz/190 g strawberries

6–7 oz/190–225 g stale wholemeal bread (weighed without crust)

Lemon juice (except with gooseberries)

2–3 pint/1.2–1.75 litre pudding basin

•METHOD•

1 Pick over the bilberries, gooseberries, blackberries or currants and wash; top and tail gooseberries or currants. Put

into a smallish saucepan with 2 oz/50 g of the sugar (do not add water) and set over very low heat for 5 minutes or until the fruit is partly submerged in juice; stir frequently until the sugar has melted. Leave to cool.

2 Pick over the raspberries and strawberries, removing mouldy raspberries and any soft patches on the strawberries. Wash and drain. Cut large strawberries in half; leave smaller ones whole. Sprinkle with the remaining 2 oz/50 g sugar. Leave for 15–20 minutes to soften.

3 Cut the bread into 6–8 slices and remove the crusts. Halve the slices and use to line the sides and bottom of the pudding basin. The bread lining must reach all the way up a 2 pint/ 1.2 litre basin or almost all the way up a larger one. Do not leave any gaps.

4 Unless using gooseberries, add a generous squeeze of lemon juice to the raspberries and strawberries. Add the cooked berries and mix gently. Spoon into the lined basin. Completely cover with a layer of bread. Place a saucer or plate on top and weight with a bag of rice or beans (if the basin is slightly too full, a little juice may overflow). Put the pudding into the refrigerator for 24 hours.

5 To turn out the pudding, slide the blade of a knife round the edge of the basin. (If the bread on top is still a little dry, it does not matter, as it will be moistened when the pudding is the other way up.) Place the basin upside-down on a serving-plate, tap the bottom and lift the basin gently.

• MICHAEL'S EXOTIC •
FRUIT SALAD

Fruit salad is never going to be cheap but it is one of the few sweets which is entirely healthy and is quick and easy – useful if you have another course or courses to prepare. Making a good one, however, needs a little thought, as it demands a balance of textures, flavours and colour; it also depends on the quality and ripeness of the fruit and the nature of the accompanying juice.

The mango will be expensive but gives the salad its character. Another possibility is pineapple, but buy small one, which is all you need. The sweetness of mangoes, on the other hand, is fairly reliable; they are at the right stage of ripeness when they smell sweet and give to the touch but are not soft. Kiwi fruit also sometimes have very little flavour but always look beautiful; when ripe, they should similarly give to the touch, but in this salad a hardish one is a good idea as it will then contribute a slight tartness. For those who dislike the bitterness of grapefruit, I have suggested substituting lime juice and slightly underripe pears. Add the juice which escapes from the fruit as you cut it to the salad. For 6.

• INGREDIENTS •

8 oz/250 g blue grapes or (in season) cherries or blackberries

1 grapefruit or ½ lime plus 2 hardish Conference pears

2 oranges

1 kiwi fruit

1 mango

2 bananas

2 apples

½ pint/300 ml unsweetened tropical fruit juice or orange juice

• METHOD •

1 Wash the grapes, cherries or blackberries and blot dry with kitchen paper. Halve grapes or cherries and remove the pips or stones. Put into a large bowl.

2 Peel the grapefruit and oranges: do not pull off the skin, which leaves a layer of pith behind, but remove it with a sharp knife. Slice, discard the pips and add the slices to the bowl. If using pears, quarter, peel and core them and cut into cubes; put into the bowl. Pour in the tropical fruit or orange juice.

3 Peel and slice the kiwi fruit, trimming off the stalk end. Peel the mango, cut into thick slices as far as the stone on each side, then cut off the flesh clinging to the stone; chop the slices into cubes and add. Peel, slice and add the bananas. Wash, dry, quarter and core the apples; cut into dice and put into the bowl. Squeeze the lime (if using) and add the juice to taste. Serve chilled.

•SPICED APPLE• YOGHURT WITH GIN

The gin adds depth and zest to the apple without being perceptible as such. The dish is quick and easy to prepare and, apart from the gin (of which you need only 3 tablespoons), very cheap. *For 6.*

• INGREDIENTS •

½ inch/1 cm piece cinnamon stick

2 lb/1 kg Bramley or similar cooking apples

4 cloves

8 oz/250 g caster or light soft brown sugar

Juice ½ small lemon

3 tablespoons gin

8 oz/250 g Greek or Greek-style yoghurt

• METHOD •

1 Crush the cinnamon. Quarter, core, peel and slice the apples. Put into a saucepan with the cinnamon, cloves and sugar (do not add water) and sweat over very low heat until the sugar has dissolved and the juice has started to run. Turn up the heat slightly and cook for 10–15 minutes or until the fruit is soft and disintegrating. If it seems very liquid, continue to cook until it is fairly thick.

2 Press through a sieve. Allow to cool. Add the lemon juice. Stir in the gin. Add to the yoghurt; stir and chill.

·WHEN YOU'RE·
REALLY BROKE

Lots of the recipes in this book are cheap: Cheese and Chilli Dip (made with Cheddar), for instance, which you can eat with crusty bread and crudités such as carrots, celery and baby turnips; Curried Lentil and Mushroom Soup (page 32) is pretty inexpensive; so is pasta with Tomato and Herb Sauce (page 35), at any rate if you grow the herbs; if you do, Pasta with Courgettes and Basil Butter (page 45) will also not cost much in the autumn when courgettes are in season. More obvious are stir-fried and curried vegetable dishes (but, please, not made only with low-protein vegetables: add at least some peas or a few nuts – or follow with cheese). Then there are pulse dishes: few items could be cheaper than Clara's Spiced Lentils (page 97), which I have also recommended for parties. Scrambled Eggs with Cheese and Chives (page 109), if you grow the chives, is both cheap and quick; and there are Coleslaw, Carrot and Peanut Salad, and Tuscan-style Bean and Tomato Salad (pages 123, 120 and 118).

Partly because of the much longer vegetarian tradition in countries where rice replaces potatoes, I have so far not given any potato recipes except one in the chapter on salads (and now potatoes for salads are relatively dear). Here, therefore, I have included several, in particular information on and recipes for baked potatoes, not because I imagine that anyone does not know how to bake a potato but to ensure that they do full justice to them and to suggest one or two new ways of stuffing them.

As yoghurt is useful as a cooking ingredient as well as to eat in its own right, I have also given directions for making your own, which, if you do it regularly, could make a worthwhile saving. I admit that adding strawberries and making yoghurt ices is not exactly economic, but have suggested them on the basis that they are cheap luxuries (and ices represent a saving in that they are a way – I think the very best way – of preserving seasonal fruit).

• LENTIL AND LEMON PÂTÉ •

Since you only need one lemon as opposed to four limes, this is rather cheaper than Clara's Lentil and Lime Pâte (page 16). I have suggested using the larger green lentils rather than brown because, although harder to mash, they have a fresher flavour.

For maximum nutritional value serve with warm, crusty bread or home-made rusks (see page 15). For 4.

• INGREDIENTS •

1 small onion	Small bunch parsley
1 large clove garlic	4 oz/125 g green lentils
1 teaspoon cumin seeds	1 tablespoon oil
2 teaspoons coriander seeds	Salt
1 small lemon	Pepper

Saucepan with a lid

• METHOD •

1 Peel and finely chop the onion and garlic. Crush the cumin and coriander seeds; squeeze the lemon. Trim the stalks off the parsley, wash it and leave it to drain in a sieve or colander. Pick over and rinse the lentils.

2 In the saucepan, fry the onion in the oil over low heat, turning often, for 8–10 minutes or until soft but not brown. Add the garlic and continue frying for 3–4 minutes; sprinkle in the spices and fry for 2–3 minutes more. Add the lentils, 1 pint/600 ml water and half the lemon juice (do not add salt at this stage). Boil fast for 2 minutes; then lower the heat until the lentils are simmering, cover and cook for 25 more minutes. Add a little salt and rather more pepper and continue cooking for 5–10 minutes or until the lentils are tender when prodded with a fork. Add a little more boiling water if necessary. If there is surplus liquid when the lentils are cooked, raise the heat a little until it has evaporated. Mash with a fork and allow to cool.

3 Finely chop and stir in the parsley. Add more lemon juice to taste: be cautious and put in only a little at a time, because if there is too much the pâté will be sharp. Adjust the seasoning after adding the lemon: you will probably need a little more salt (in this recipe particularly, the right balance of seasoning makes an enormous difference).

•ONION AND TOMATO SOUP•

Piero Amodio, owner of the Coffee Gallery, near the British Museum in London, is a particularly brilliant source of ideas for soups. This is based on another of his recipes, although it is somewhat different from the original. Like Onion and Courgette Quiche, the soup depends on frying the onions to just the right shade of brown.

Serve with crusty bread. *For 3.*

•INGREDIENTS•

4 oz/125 g butter beans, soaked overnight in cold water

Salt

1½ lb/750 g onions

1 lb/500 g ripe tomatoes

2 tablespoons oil

Pepper

2 tablespoons tomato purée

Small saucepan with a lid
Wok or large saucepan

•METHOD•

1 Drain, rinse and pick over the beans. Put into the small saucepan with quite a lot of fresh water (do not add salt) and bring to the boil. Skim, boil fast for 5 minutes, cover and simmer for 45 minutes. Add a little salt and continue to simmer for 5–10 more minutes or until just tender. Drain over a bowl; keep the cooking liquor.

2 Peel the onions and slice them into fine rings. Peel and chop the tomatoes.

3 Fry the onions in the oil over low heat in the wok or large saucepan for 25–35 minutes or until an even mid-brown: stir every now and again for the first 20 minutes and constantly for the last 5–15 minutes. You can speed them up by raising the heat a little towards the end. Add the tomatoes, season fairly generously with salt and pepper and simmer for 7–10 minutes, pressing the flesh against the bottom of the pan until liquified. Stir in the tomato purée. Make up the bean liquor to 1 pint/ 600 ml with cold water and add to the wok or pan with the beans. Simmer for 20 minutes.

• PIERO'S BEAN AND •
GARLIC SOUP

This is about as cheap and simple as you can get – but you have to like garlic (and so do your friends: be warned). You need enough for it almost to burn the tongue.

If possible, serve in deep individual bowls; otherwise, use one large bowl. *For 3–4.*

• INGREDIENTS •

2 medium onions

2 tablespoons olive oil

8 oz/250 g haricot beans, soaked overnight in cold water

Salt

Pepper

3–4 slices wholemeal bread (weighing about 1½ oz/40 g each without crust)

8–10 fat cloves garlic

3–4 oz/90–125 g Parmesan cheese to serve

Wok or large saucepan with a lid

• METHOD •

1 Peel and finely chop the onions. Fry in about 1½ table-spoons oil in the wok or large saucepan over low heat for 12–15 minutes or until beginning to change colour.

2 Drain and rinse the beans and add to the onions with 2 pints/1 litre fresh cold water (do not add salt). Bring to the boil and boil fast for 5 minutes. Reduce the heat, cover and simmer for 40–50 minutes or until the beans are tender when prodded with a fork. Add 1 teaspoon salt and a little pepper and simmer for 10–15 minutes more.

3 Cut the crusts from the bread. Peel and roughly chop the garlic, then crush as finely as possible with 2 teaspoons oil. Spread an equal quantity over each slice of bread. Put the bread into the bottom of the serving-bowls or large bowl.

4 Grate the Parmesan. Bring the soup to a sharp boil and pour over the bread in the bowl(s). Leave for a few minutes for the bread to soak and the flavour of the garlic to permeate the soup. Serve the Parmesan separately.

• CABBAGE CHEESE •

This is really quick. It does not take long to prepare the ingredients and the cabbage cooks in 7–10 minutes.

As it is not very substantial, although satisfying at the time, serve it with bread, mashed potato, Baked Potato (see page 167), or Polenta (see page 128). For 2.

• INGREDIENTS •

4 oz/125 g button mushrooms	8 oz/250 g green cabbage
4 cloves garlic	1 tablespoon oil
1½ oz/40 g Parmesan or 2 oz/50 g Cheddar cheese	Salt
	Pepper

Saucepan with a lid

• METHOD •

1 Trim the stalks of the mushrooms; wash the mushrooms, blot dry with kitchen paper and slice finely. Peel and finely slice the garlic. Grate the cheese.

2 Discard the outermost leaves of the cabbage, cut into ½ inch/1 cm slices, removing the central stem and any other thick pieces of stalk, and wash.

3 Warm the oil over medium heat in the saucepan. Add the garlic and fry for about 30 seconds or until just starting to change colour. Add the mushrooms and fry for 3–4 minutes or until soft, stirring continuously. Add ½ pint/300 ml water and the cabbage. Season lightly with salt and more generously with pepper, cover and steam for 6 minutes. Test the cabbage by cutting with a knife and continue to cook for 1–3 minutes or until just tender but still crisp. Drain and sprinkle immediately with the cheese; Cheddar will melt with the heat of the cabbage and coat the leaves almost like a thin sauce. Eat at once.

•ALL ABOUT•
BAKED POTATOES

Baking potatoes is so easy that you probably never think about it except in terms of possible stuffings. However, as is usual with simple dishes, details make all the difference.

For a soft, crumbly interior, you need floury potatoes. In supermarkets, potatoes are usually labelled with the variety and the uses for which they are suitable, but at greengrocers' they may not be labelled at all. The kinds to choose at different times of the year are: Maris Bard and Spunta (June and July); Estima, Marfona, Wilja (August–March); Cara, Desirée, Golden Wonder, Kerr's Pink, Maris Piper, Pentland Crown, Pentland Dell, Pentland Squire and Romano (September–May).

If the potato is to be served with something else, a 6–8 oz/190–250 g one is large enough for one person, but if it is to be a whole meal, 14 oz–1 lb/440–500 g is the weight to buy.

To prepare the potatoes, scrub them and pare off any green patches, where chlorophyll has formed as a result of exposure to light and which are toxic, and cut out eyes and sprouts (cutting the skin will not spoil them when baked, as a crisp crust will form). Pricking with a fork or skewer to prevent the skin bursting is generally recommended, although in my experience hardly necessary, as this very seldom happens. You can bake them just as they are, but if you want a crisp, brown skin paint them with oil (if you have no pastry-brush, rub them with oiled greaseproof paper). Lay the potatoes a little apart on a baking-sheet covered with aluminium foil and bake in a pre-heated oven at 400°F, 200°C, Gas Mark 6, or 425°F, 220°C, Gas Mark 7, for 50–60 minutes for 8 oz/250 g potatoes, or for 1¼–1½ hours for those weighing about 1 lb/500 g; the higher oven heat will save about 5 minutes for the smaller size, 10 minutes for the larger. They can also be cooked at a lower heat: at 350°F, 180°C, Gas Mark 4, 8 oz/250 g potatoes will take about 1½ hours. They are cooked when soft all the way through: test with a skewer or sharp knife.

It would be possible to fill a separate book with suggestions for stuffings, and anyway everyone has their own favourites. However, as in my view part of the attraction of baked potatoes is that they are a lazy option, I have given just a few fairly simple ones.

• CREAMY GORGONZOLA • POTATO

This does not taste strongly of Gorgonzola but the cheese gives the potato an unexpectedly melting, creamy texture. Do not forget the nutmeg, which is especially effective with Gorgonzola. Allow an extra 20 minutes for baking the filling after the potato is cooked.

Serve with watercress or chicory and watercress. For 1.

• INGREDIENTS •

1 *baking potato weighing about*
1 lb/500 g

A little oil

3 *oz/90 g Gorgonzola cheese*

2 *tablespoons milk*

Nutmeg

Small baking-sheet

• METHOD •

Paint the potato lightly with oil and bake as described opposite;
do not turn off the oven when it is ready. Halve it lengthways as
soon as it is cool enough to handle. Scoop out the flesh, leaving
a margin of about ½ inch/1 cm next to the skin. Mash the
Gorgonzola with a fork, add to the potato flesh with the milk
and beat smooth. Pile back into the skins (there will be almost
too much) and grate a generous sprinkling of nutmeg over the
top. Return to the oven and bake for 20 minutes or until
showing signs of browning.

• POLLY'S LEMON •
AND MUSHROOM POTATO

The lemon and mushroom make this very light and sum-
mery; the turnips add crispness. *For* 1.

• INGREDIENTS •

1 baking potato weighing about
1 lb/500 g

About 1½ tablespoons oil

4 oz/125 g button mushrooms

2 baby turnips

1 clove garlic

½ inch/1 cm piece fresh root ginger

½ lemon

1 tablespoon dark soy sauce

Small baking-sheet

• METHOD •

1 Paint the potato lightly with oil and bake (see page 168).
Trim the mushroom stalks; wash the mushrooms, dry on kitchen
paper and slice finely. Peel and halve the turnips, cutting out
the stalk indentation, and chop into matchsticks about
¼ inch/5 mm wide. Keep the mushrooms and turnips separate.
Peel and finely slice the garlic and ginger. Cut a wedge from the
½ lemon for a garnish; squeeze the juice from the remainder.

2 As soon as the potato is cool enough to handle, slash the top diagonally across into 4, then slash lengthways to make 8 'segments' without cutting right through. Set the soy sauce within easy reach. Warm 1½ tablespoons oil over high heat, put in the garlic and ginger and allow to fry until beginning to change colour. Add the turnips and stir continuously for 1 minute. Add the mushrooms and continue stirring for 1–2 minutes. Stir in the soy sauce and remove from the heat. Add a little of the lemon juice. Pull the segments of potato apart enough to stuff with the filling and sprinkle a little more lemon juice over the top. Serve with the reserved lemon wedge and add more juice to taste.

• AVOCADO AND •
PEAR POTATO

The idea of combining avocado pear and pear comes from a recipe supplied by the Potato Marketing Board.

The avocado should give slightly all over; the pear should also give, but only very slightly. This recipe calls for Yoghurt Cheese (see page 180). For 2.

• INGREDIENTS •

2 *baking potatoes weighing about*
1 lb/500 g each

1 tablespoon olive oil, plus a
little extra

1 stick celery

1 tablespoon wine vinegar

4 *tablespoons Yoghurt Cheese*
(see page 180)

1 slightly underripe Comice or
Conference pear

1 small avocado pear

Small baking-sheet

• METHOD •

1 Paint the potatoes with a little oil and bake as described on page 168. Trim the root and leaf ends of the celery, pare off any brown streaks, wash and blot dry; slice finely. Gradually stir 1 tablespoon oil and the vinegar into the cheese and beat to a smooth, thick sauce. Quarter, core, peel and finely chop the pear; mix with the celery into the cheese. Halve, stone and peel the avocado pear, slice finely and stir gently into the cheese mixture.

2 Slash the potato into 8 segments as described in stage 2 of Polly's Lemon and Mushroom Potato (page 169–70), pull slightly apart and pile the stuffing into the slits and over the top.

• BAKED POTATO • WITH EGG AND CHIVES

Bake the potato and slit open as described in stage 2 of Polly's Lemon and Mushroom Potato (page 169-70). Make Scrambled Eggs with Cheese and Chives (see page 109), pile into the slits and over the top. Serve with green salad. *For* 1.

• ALEX'S NORMANDY • POTATOES

This is so light and creamy that it is difficult to believe that it is only potatoes in an onion and cheese sauce. There are two ways of making it. Alex cooks the raw slices of potato in the sauce, which means stirring almost continuously for 20–25 minutes to ensure that the sauce does not stick to the bottom of the pan, but which saves washing up an extra saucepan. The much quicker alternative is to boil the potatoes separately and stir them into the sauce just before baking. Potatoes with a waxy texture are preferable, such as Alcmaria, Arran Comet or Pentland Javelin.

Serve alone or with a plainly cooked vegetable like cabbage, broccoli or Brussels sprouts. *For* 2 *if eaten alone or* 3 *if with a vegetable.*

• INGREDIENTS •

1 lb/500 g potatoes	½ oz/15 g butter
Salt	1 tablespoon oil
2 medium onions	1 oz/25 g flour
1 dried chilli	Pepper
1 pint/600 ml milk	3 oz/90 g Cheddar cheese
1 oz/25 g Parmesan cheese	

**Shallow ovenware dish about 12 inches/30 cm long
and 8½ inches/22 cm wide**

• METHOD •

1 Scrub the potatoes, peel off any green patches and cut out eyes and sprouts. Slice very thinly. The quality of the dish depends on the slices being really thin. If you are going to boil them separately, just cover with slightly salted water, bring to the boil and boil gently for 4–5 minutes or until just (but only just) tender, then drain.

2 Peel the onions and slice into very thin rounds. Wash and dry the chilli, trim the stalk end, remove all the seeds and dice the flesh as finely as possible. Do not touch your eyes while chopping it and wash your hands immediately afterwards.

3 Heat but do not boil the milk. Grate the Parmesan. Melt the butter in the oil over low heat and fry the onion for 8–10 minutes or until soft but not brown. Add the chilli and fry for 2–3 minutes. Stir in the flour. As soon as it is absorbed, pour in the milk slowly, stirring continuously; keep stirring until it has thickened into a sauce. Season lightly with salt and more generously with pepper and add the potatoes. If they are already cooked, simmer for 3–4 minutes and remove from the heat. If they are uncooked, simmer for 20–25 minutes, stirring very frequently, until they are just soft. Stir in the Parmesan.

4 Pre-heat the oven to 400°F, 200°C, Gas Mark 6. Lightly grease the ovenware dish. Pour in the hot potatoes and sauce. Grate the Cheddar and sprinkle over the top. Bake in the oven for 20–25 minutes or until golden and bubbling.

•POTATO PANCAKES WITH•
YOGHURT CHEESE

In these, instead of making a pancake and stuffing it, you grate the 'stuffing' and incorporate it into the batter. The chief point about the pancakes is that they should be fried really crisp, eaten very hot and accompanied by thick, creamy, chilled Yoghurt Cheese (see page 180).

As a smooth surface prevents the pancakes from sticking, use a non-stick frying-pan if possible; this will also mean that you need less oil. Leave the batter to stand for 30 minutes–1 hour before cooking, as this will give the starch granules time to swell. Use floury potatoes, such as King Edward, Cara or Marfona.

In the interests of crispness, eat the pancakes at once, as soon as they are fried, even though this means that everyone cannot be served simultaneously. For 3–4.

Beetroot will make the pancakes a wonderful deep pink.

• INGREDIENTS •

1 lb/500 g floury potatoes	Salt
8 oz/250 g carrots, or raw beetroot	Pepper
1 largish onion	3 tablespoons plus 1 teaspoon oil
2 oz/50 g wholemeal flour	Yoghurt Cheese made with
4 eggs (size 2 or 3)	1 lb/500 g yoghurt (see page 180)

Non-stick frying-pan
Fish-slice

• METHOD •

1 Peel the potatoes, onions and carrots. If using beetroot, scrub it, cover with salted water and boil for 50 minutes–1 hour or until tender; peel as soon as it is cool enough to handle. Coarsely grate all the vegetables and leave in a sieve to drain.

2 Put the flour into a bowl and make a well in the middle. Add and beat in the eggs one by one. Stir in ⅔ teaspoon salt, a generous grinding of pepper and 1 teaspoon oil. Leave to stand for 30 minutes–1 hour.

3 Mix the grated vegetables with the batter. Warm 1 table-spoon oil over medium to lowish heat in the frying-pan and add 1 heaped tablespoon of the batter mixture. Flatten it so that the pancake will be thin (the thinner the pancake, the crisper it will be). If there is room in the pan, add another. Fry for 1–2 minutes or until the undersides are firm and brown (lift the corner with the fish-slice to check), then turn and fry until the other sides are brown. Serve at once. Flick out or wipe off any browned remnants of batter or vegetables in the pan and repeat. If using a non-stick pan, you will need to replenish the oil only after every second set of pancakes. Continue until the batter is finished: there should be enough for 10 smallish pancakes. Serve with Yoghurt Cheese taken from the refrigerator just before serving.

• YOGHURT •

As bought yoghurt costs more than twice as much as milk and the ingredients are simply milk plus a small amount of yoghurt, the saving on making your own is over 100 per cent. Very little work is involved but, as with bread, you have to allow time for a living organism to reproduce – in this case 6–8 hours. Unlike bread, the home-made version, which depends chiefly on the yoghurt used as a starter for its quality, will not differ much from the yoghurt you buy: an enormous difference, however, can be made by adding your own flavourings.

The only equipment you need is a saucepan, spoon, pudding basin or other heat-proof bowl and (since, like yeast, the yoghurt bacteria need warmth) a larger bowl and a towel for insulation. As not only the yoghurt but also other bacteria flourish in warm milk, you should sterilise the equipment by rinsing in boiling water. If you use ordinary milk, this will also need sterilising: it is therefore more practical to use UHT. (To sterilise ordinary milk, simmer for 10 minutes.)

Any yoghurt can be used as a starter provided that it is unflavoured, fresh (that is, not near its sell-by date) and unpasteurised – which includes most of the brands on sale; pasteurised yoghurts can be distinguished by their relatively long sell-by dates. You do not need to buy yoghurt specifically labelled 'live' (which merely means unpasteurised). The flavour of the starter yoghurt, however, is important because yours will be similar: if you want mild yoghurt, choose a mild starter. It can be full- or low-fat, as you wish. The milk used can also be full- or low-fat according to the kind of yoghurt you want.

As well as adding flavourings of various kinds, you can use home-made (or, if it comes to that, commercial) yoghurt for making fruit ices and yoghurt cheese. *Makes just over 1 lb/500 g (enough for 4).*

• INGREDIENTS •

1 *tablespoon*   1 *pint*/600 *ml* UHT *milk*
unpasteurised yoghurt

Pudding basin or similar heat-proof bowl
Large bowl
Towel

• METHOD •

1 To sterilise the equipment, fill a saucepan with water (there must be enough water to fill the pudding basin in turn). Put a tablespoon into the water, bring to the boil and boil for at least 1 minute. Pour quickly into the basin; also transfer the spoon (use a cloth as the handle may be hot). Let the water stand for a few minutes. Empty, leaving the spoon in the basin, and allow the basin to cool, preferably until it is lukewarm rather than cold.

2 Put the yoghurt into the basin and stir until smooth with the sterilised spoon. Pour the milk into the saucepan. Wash your hands (because of the need to test its temperature) and heat the milk until it feels positively warm to the touch but not hot. Ideally it should be 107°F/42°C: a little deviation on either side does not matter, but if it is much hotter the yoghurt may curdle, and if much cooler, little will happen and the yoghurt will remain unsatisfactorily thin. Mix 1 tablespoon of the milk with the yoghurt, then pour in the rest slowly, stirring continuously. Keep stirring for a minute or two. Cover with a plate and set the basin in the large bowl. Using a teapot, pour into the large bowl enough water of about the same temperature as the milk to come three-quarters of the way up the basin: take care not to add too much or it may overflow into the yoghurt. Wrap in a towel and leave in a warm place for 6–8 hours or until the yoghurt is set. Do not leave longer or the yoghurt may be very sharp, or even curdle. If the basin is still warm, cool by standing in cold water. Keep covered and store in the refrigerator.

The yoghurt will keep for up to 4 days and can be used as a starter for a new batch for the first 2 days. If it is older, contamination by other bacteria is more likely. It should be replaced as a starter by a commercial yoghurt after 3 batches.

• FLAVOURED YOGHURT •

The number of possible flavourings that can be added to yoghurt is almost unlimited. Below are 6 of the simplest and (in my view) the best. *For 1 lb/500 g yoghurt.*

• HONEY •

Thick honey is more difficult to mix with yoghurt than the runny sort but runny honey will make the yoghurt too liquid.

• INGREDIENTS •

3 *tablespoons thick honey*   A *few almonds (optional)*

• METHOD •

Stir the honey into the yoghurt. If using almonds, split or roughly chop them and toast briefly in the oven (5–6 minutes at 200°C, 400°F, Gas Mark 6) or in a thick saucepan (3–4 minutes over moderate heat); scatter over the top of the yoghurt.

• LEMON •

• INGREDIENTS •

About 3 oz/90 g caster sugar   Juice 1 small lemon

• METHOD •

Mix the sugar with the yoghurt. Add the lemon juice, taste and add more sugar if needed.

• RASPBERRY OR STRAWBERRY •

• INGREDIENTS •

8 oz/250 g strawberries or   Squeeze of lemon juice
6 oz/190 g raspberries   (if using strawberries)

About 3 oz/90 g caster sugar

• METHOD •

Pick over and wash the fruit. Leave to drain on a plate lined with kitchen paper.

If using strawberries, chop them, sprinkle with the sugar and leave for a few minutes for the juice to run, then add to the yoghurt with the lemon juice.

If using raspberries, sprinkle them with the sugar, leave for a few minutes, then crush lightly with a fork before adding to the yoghurt.

• BANANA •

• INGREDIENTS •

2 bananas   3 oz/90 g soft brown sugar

• METHOD •

Mash the bananas with the sugar and mix with the yoghurt.

• Vanilla •

Use a fresh vanilla pod (available from good grocers) rather than essence. The pod will be relatively expensive but can be used twice. It must be heated with the milk before the yoghurt is made.

• INGREDIENTS •

1 vanilla pod   1½–2 oz/40–50 g caster sugar

• METHOD •

Rinse the pod in cold water and score the surface lengthways with a knife. Add to the milk, bring to the boil, then leave to cool for 15–20 minutes or until just warm. Remove the pod, wash, dry and keep for a second use; if possible, store it in an airtight jar once dry. Make the yoghurt. Add sugar to taste after it has set.

• Yoghurt Ices •

Excellent fruit ices can be made with yoghurt. In fact, some fruit tastes better in ices made with yoghurt than with cream. It is important, however, to use whole-milk rather than low-fat yoghurt, because without a machine to break them up, coarse ice-crystals will form as low-fat yoghurt freezes.

Ices should be frozen in plastic containers with fitted lids. Those in which bought ices or other frozen foods are sold are fine. As a last resort, use a pudding basin covered with foodwrap (but make sure that the foodwrap is sealed round the rim).

The ices taste better if eaten fairly soon after you make them, but you can keep them for 2–3 months; after that the flavour deteriorates. Allow 1–2 hours for thawing and mix or beat with a fork before serving. The following quantities make about 12 oz/375 g (enough for 4–6).

•GOOSEBERRY, BILBERRY• BLACKCURRANT AND DAMSON ICES

Just as they make excellent jam, so damsons also make remarkably good ices: gooseberries are also especially recommended for their full flavour.

With damsons, 6 oz/190 g sugar is needed; for gooseberries, 5 oz/150 g; for bilberries and blackcurrants, 4 oz/125 g. The mildness of the yoghurt also helps to take the edge off these high-acid fruits.

• INGREDIENTS •

1 lb/500 g fruit

4–6 oz/125–190 g caster sugar

¼ pint/150 ml Greek or other mild yoghurt

• METHOD •

1 Pick over the fruit, removing any green or mouldy bilberries or currants, and wash. Leave to drain.

2 Put with the sugar (no water) over very low heat and sweat until the sugar has dissolved and the juice has started to run; turn up the heat slightly and stew for 5–6 minutes or until the fruit is soft and submerged in liquid (damsons will take 7–10 minutes). Allow to cool.

3 Pulp through a sieve and add to the yoghurt, not vice versa: yoghurt will not mix in at all well if it is added to the juice. Mix and for best results sieve again.

4 Turn into a freezer container or pudding basin and freeze for 2–2½ hours or until the edges are frozen but the centre still soft (freezing times vary according not only to the temperature of the freezer but also to the size and shape of the container – a flat, rectangular one will freeze quickest). Whisk or beat with a fork until homogenous and refreeze (this will give a slightly smoother result than without beating but is not essential). For immediate consumption, the ice will be ready after a further 1½–2 hours.

•Yoghurt Cheese•

Yoghurt cheese is simply concentrated yoghurt, and involves no more than leaving the yoghurt to drain in a sieve lined with a sterilised cloth. The obvious cloth to use is cheesecloth, which is fairly easy to buy but costs several pounds. It can be used over and over again, but must be laundered and boiled for 10 minutes before each use. A cheaper alternative is a thin (old?) tea-towel, which also needs boiling for 10 minutes; an easier option is a new J-cloth, which is ready-sterilised (packs of 5 cloths cost less than £1 at the time of writing).

The drained yoghurt is thick, creamy and has a cheese-like tartness. How tart it is will depend on the flavour of the yoghurt used as a starter and whether you drain it in or out of the refrigerator: the yoghurt bacteria will continue to multiply in a warm atmosphere, so if you want a mild result and have the space, drain it inside. Commercial pasteurised yoghurt is obviously not affected by this rule.

You can use low-fat or whole-milk yoghurt, but the lower percentage of solids in low-fat means that you will end up with far less cheese: 1 lb/500 g whole-milk yoghurt will give about 10 oz/310 g cheese, the same quantity of low-fat yoghurt only about 6 oz/190 g. Its thickness depends on how long you leave it to drain: 6 hours will give a thick cream, 8 hours the consistency of soft cheese, 10–12 hours the consistency of quite stiff cheese.

If you like, you can add a pinch of salt to the yoghurt before draining, but the cheese has a fairly positive flavour without it; for the same reason, other flavourings such as herbs do not seem to me an improvement.

The cheese is delicious as a sauce instead of yoghurt and can be served with sweet dishes in place of cream. It also makes an excellent, thick salad dressing (see page 112).

·NUTRITION·

·ENERGY AND PROTEIN·

According to the Department of Health's *Dietary Reference Values for Food, Energy and Nutrients in the United Kingdom*, published in 1991, estimated average daily needs for energy and protein are as follows:

	Kcal	Protein
18-year-olds		
Boys	2,755	46 g
Girls	2,110	37 g
19–49-year-olds		
Men	2,550	44 g
Women	1,940	36 g

These, however, are only average needs, which means that many people will require more. To be sure of obtaining enough protein, recommended amounts for the 18–49 age group are: boys and men, 55 g; girls and women, 45 g.

Proteins, which are necessary for the growth, maintenance and healing of body tissues, are composed of amino acids in different proportions and arrangements. The proportions in animal proteins are similar to man's and therefore said to have a high biological value, while those in plants are different and said to have a low value: to raise it, you need to eat more than one kind at roughly the same time. Soya is exceptional in having a high value and is thus of especial importance to vegans.

A point about protein which should perhaps be stressed is that even if you eat the recommended amount and are careful about combining plant proteins, you will not utilise it for its longer-term purposes if you run yourself short of calories, since it will be burnt up instead of fats or carbohydrates for energy.

Besides protein you need 12 different vitamins, a large number of minerals (but most of them in minute quantities) and fibre. Anyone who eats a variety of fresh (or frozen) and some wholegrain foods will almost certainly obtain more than enough of all of them, but recommended daily amounts for men and women aged 19–49 of the main vitamins plus calcium, iron and sodium are given below, with brief comments on their functions. For foods containing them, see the table on page 184.

• VITAMIN A •

Promotes healthy skin, hair and eyes. Men need 700 μg; women, 600 μg.

• B VITAMINS •

The B group of vitamins is needed to metabolise various constituents of food. B1 is required for carbohydrate; B2 for protein, fat and carbohydrate; B3 to maintain levels of sugar and cholesterol in the blood. B12 is needed to metabolise some amino acids and by the nervous system: lack leads to a certain type of anaemia and to permanent neurological damage. The chief sources of it are animal foods, such as milk and eggs, but some bacteria and hence fermented products, like miso and yeast extract, which are permissible for vegans, also contain it.

• VITAMIN B1 (THIAMIN) •

Men need 1 mg; women, 0.9 mg.

• VITAMIN B2 (RIBOFLAVIN) •

Men need 1.3 mg; women, 1.1 mg.

• VITAMIN B3 (NIACIN) •

Men need 16.5 mg; women, 13 mg.

• VITAMIN B12 •

Men and women need 1.5 μg.

• VITAMIN C •

Promotes healing; prevents scurvy. Men and women need 40 mg.

• VITAMIN D •

Maintains levels of phosphorus and potassium in the blood. The most important source is sunlight; if you lead a normal life and are outside reasonably often, you do not need further supplies via food.

• CALCIUM •

Needed to form bones and teeth. Men need 1,000 mg; women, 800 mg.

• IRON •

Needed for the formation of red blood cells which carry oxygen around the body; lack leads to anaemia. Men need 8.7 mg; women (because of having to compensate for that lost in menstruation) 14.8 mg.

• SODIUM AND CHLORINE •

Sodium chloride = salt; needed to maintain water balance and for nerve and muscle function. Exertion involving much sweating raises the amount needed: otherwise, both men and women need about 3 g.

• FIBRE •

Fibre is obtained from plant cellulose, a good source of which is husks and bran, one reason for preferring whole to refined foods.

However, you are recommended to avoid excessive amounts, so that to use white rice or flour for some purposes is not deleterious.

• SUGAR •

Sugar which occurs naturally as part of foods such as fruit does not harm the teeth; added sugar (both brown and white) and honey does.

• CHOLESTEROL •

For most people, cholesterol in food is not a major factor in blood cholesterol: more important is the amount of saturated fat eaten. You are advised not to eat more than 30% of your total calorie intake in the form of fat and not more than 10%, i.e. about 200 kcal, in the form of saturated fat. The chief sources of saturated fat in a vegetarian diet are oil and butter, cream and cheese. Double cream, for instance, contains 30 g per 100 g;

• FOOD VALUES •

Except where marked*, all figures are taken from a report by the Ministry of Agriculture, Fisheries and Food (HMSO, 1985).

Composition per 100 g (raw edible weight except where stated)

Food	Energy kcal	Protein g	Fat g	Carbo-hydrate (as mono-saccharide) g
MILK				
Cream – double	447	1.5	48.2	2.0
Milk, liquid, whole	65	3.2	3.9	4.6
Milk, liquid, skimmed	32	3.4	0.1	4.7
Yoghurt, low fat, natural	65	5.1	0.8	10.0
CHEESE				
Cheddar	406	26.0	33.5	0
Cottage	96	13.6	4.0	1.4
Feta	245	16.5	19.9	0

Cheddar cheese, 22 g per 100 g; sunflower oil, 12 g per 100 g; and olive oil 14 g per 100 g.

• PROCESSING OF FOODS •

Freezing has little effect on vitamins and minerals. Frozen fruit and vegetables (unless partly cooked before freezing) are therefore almost as nutritious as fresh ones.

Any heat processing such as canning will reduce vitamin C and thiamin content.

Drying destroys about half the vitamin C content. If sulphur dioxide is added, all thiamin will also be destroyed.

Calcium mg	Iron mg	Sodium mg	Vitamin A (retinol) equivalent) μg	Thia- min mg	Ribo- flavin mg	Niacin equivalent mg	Vitamin C mg
50	0.2	30	500	0.02	0.08	0.4	1
103	0.1	50	56	0.05	0.17	0.9	1.5
108	0.1	50	1	0.05	0.18	0.9	1.5
200	0.1	80	12	0.06	0.25	1.2	0.8
800	0.4	610	363	0.04	0.50	6.2	0
60	0.1	450	41	0.02	0.19	3.3	0
384	0.2	1,260	270	0.03	0.11	4.2	0

Composition per 100 g (raw edible weight except where stated)

Food	Energy kcal	Protein g	Fat g	Carbo-hydrate (as mono-saccharide) g
EGGS				
Eggs, boiled	147	12.3	10.9	0
FATS				
Butter	740	0.4	82.0	0
Margarine, average	730	0.1	81.0	0
Cooking and salad oil	899	0	99.9	0
PRESERVES, ETC.				
Honey	288	0.4	0	76.4
Jam	262	0.5	0	69.2
Marmalade	261	0.1	0	69.5
Sugar, white	394	0	0	105.3
VEGETABLES AND PULSES				
Aubergines	14	0.7	0	3.1
Baked beans	81	4.8	0.6	15.1
*Beans, cannellini	340	22	2	61
Beans, runner, boiled	19	1.9	0.2	2.7
Beans, red kidney, raw	272	22.1	1.7	45.0
Beans, soya, boiled	141	12.4	6.4	9.0
Beetroot	44	1.8	0	9.9
Brussels sprouts, boiled	18	2.8	0	1.7
Cabbage, raw	22	2.8	0	2.8
Cabbage, boiled	15	1.7	0	2.3
Carrots, old	23	0.7	0	5.4
Cauliflower, cooked	9	1.6	0	0.8
Celery	8	0.9	0	1.3
Courgettes, raw	29	1.6	0.4	5.0
Cucumber	10	0.6	0.1	1.8
Lentils, cooked	99	7.6	0.5	17.0
Lettuce	12	1.0	0.4	1.2
Mushrooms	13	1.8	0.6	0
Onion	23	0.9	0	5.2
Parsnips, cooked	56	1.3	0	13.5
Peas, frozen, boiled	72	6.0	0.9	10.7
Peppers, green	12	0.9	0	2.2
Potatoes	74	2.0	0.2	17.1

Calcium mg	Iron mg	Sodium mg	Vitamin A (retinol) equivalent) μg	Thia-min mg	Ribo-flavin mg	Niacin equivalent mg	Vitamin C mg
52	2.0	140	190	0.09	0.47	3.7	0
15	0.2	870	985	0	0	0.1	0
4	0.3	800	860	0	0	0.1	0
0	0	0	0	0	0	0	0
5	0.4	11	0	0	0.05	0.2	0
18	1.2	14	2	0	0	0	10
35	0.6	18	8	0	0	0	10
2	0	0	0	0	0	0	0
10	0.4	3	0	0.05	0.03	1.0	5
48	1.4	550	12	0.08	0.06	1.3	0
–	–	10	–	–	–	–	–
22	0.7	1	67	0.03	0.07	0.8	5
140	6.7	40	0	0.54	0.18	5.5	0
145	2.5	15	0	0.26	0.16	3.4	0
30	0.4	64	0	0.02	0.04	0.4	5
25	0.5	2	67	0.06	0.10	0.9	40
57	0.6	7	50	0.06	0.05	0.8	55
38	0.4	4	50	0.03	0.03	0.5	20
48	0.6	95	2,000	0.06	0.05	0.7	6
18	0.4	4	5	0.06	0.06	0.8	20
52	0.6	140	0	0.03	0.03	0.5	7
30	1.5	1	58	0.05	0.09	0.6	16
23	0.3	13	0	0.04	0.04	0.3	8
13	2.4	12	3	0.11	0.04	1.6	0
23	0.9	9	167	0.07	0.08	0.4	15
3	1.0	9	0	0.10	0.40	4.6	3
31	0.3	10	0	0.03	0.05	0.4	10
36	0.5	4	0	0.07	0.06	0.9	10
35	1.6	2	50	0.30	0.09	1.6	12
9	0.4	2	33	0.08	0.03	0.9	100
8	0.4	8	0	0.20	0.02	1.5	8–19

Composition per 100 g (raw edible weight except where stated)

Food	Energy kcal	Protein g	Fat g	Carbo- hydrate (as mono- saccharide) g
Spinach, boiled	30	5.1	0.5	1.4
Sweet potato	91	1.2	0.6	21.5
Tomatoes, fresh	14	0.9	0	2.8
Turnips, cooked	14	0.7	0.3	2.3
Watercress	14	2.9	0	0.7
FRUIT				
Apples	46	0.3	0	11.9
Apricots, dried	182	4.8	0	43.4
Avocado pear	223	4.2	22.2	1.8
Bananas	76	1.1	0	19.2
Blackcurrants	28	0.9	0	6.6
Gooseberries, cooked, unsweetened	14	0.9	0	2.9
Grapes	63	0.6	0	16.1
Grapefruit	22	0.6	0	5.3
Oranges	35	0.8	0	8.5
Orange juice	38	0.6	0	9.4
Peaches	37	0.6	0	9.1
Pears	41	0.3	0	10.6
Plums	32	0.6	0.	7.9
Prunes, dried	161	2.4	0	40.3
Raspberries	25	0.9	0	5.6
Strawberries	26	0.6	0	6.2
Sultanas	250	1.8	0	64.7
NUTS AND SEEDS				
Almonds	565	16.9	53.5	4.3
*Cashew nuts (salted)	561	17	46	29
*Chestnuts	194	3	2	42
Coconut, desiccated	604	5.6	62.0	6.4
*Hazelnuts	634	13	62	17
Peanuts, roasted and salted	570	24.3	49.0	8.6
*Pecans	687	9	71	15.0
*Sunflower seeds	582	240	47.3	16.0
*Walnuts	651	15	64	16

Calcium mg	Iron mg	Sodium mg	Vitamin A (retinol equivalent) μg	Thia-min mg	Ribo-flavin mg	Niacin equivalent mg	Vitamin C mg
136	4.0	120	1,000	0.07	0.15	1.8	25
22	0.7	19	4,000†	0.10	0.06	1.2	25
13	0.4	3	100	0.06	0.04	0.8	20
55	0.4	28	0	0.03	0.04	0.6	17
220	1.6	60	500	0.10	0.10	1.1	60
4	0.3	2	5	0.04	0.02	0.1	5
92	4.1	56	600	0	0.2	3.8	0
15	1.5	2	17	0.10	0.10	1.8	15
7	0.4	1	33	0.04	0.07	0.8	10
60	1.3	3	33	0.03	0.06	0.4	200
24	0.3	2	25	0.03	0.03	0.5	31
19	0.3	2	0	0.04	0.02	0.3	4
17	0.3	1	0	0.05	0.02	0.3	40
41	0.3	3	8	0.10	0.03	0.3	50
12	0.3	2	8	0.08	0.02	0.3	25–45
5	0.4	3	83	0.02	0.05	1.1	8
8	0.2	2	2	0.03	0.03	0.3	3
12	0.3	2	37	0.05	0.03	0.6	3
38	2.9	12	160	0.10	0.20	1.9	0
41	1.2	3	13	0.02	0.03	0.5	25
22	0.7	2	5	0.02	0.03	0.5	60
52	1.8	53	5	0.10	0.08	0.6	0
250	4.2	6	0	0.24	0.92	4.7	0
35	6.2	200	–	0.41	0.16	1.3	0
46	0.9	6	–	0.14	0.02	0.5	trace
22	3.6	28	0	0.06	0.04	1.8	0
140	3.2	2	–	0.43	0.16	1.1	0
61	2.0	440	0	0.23	0.10	21.3	0
61	2.2	trace	–	0.71	0.15	1.4	0
110	6.4	–	–	1.60	0.19	4.1	0
94	2.9	2	–	0.40	0.14	1.2	0

†The vitamin A content of white and yellow varieties may vary between 0 and 12,000 μg

Composition per 100 g (raw edible weight except where stated)

Food	Energy kcal	Protein g	Fat g	Carbo-hydrate (as mono-saccharide) g
CEREALS				
Bread, brown	217	8.4	2.0	44.2
Bread, white	230	8.2	1.7	48.6
Bread, wholemeal	215	9.0	2.5	41.6
Muesli	368	12.9	7.5	66.2
Flour, white	337	9.4	1.3	76.7
Flour, wholemeal	306	12.7	2.2	62.8
Rice, raw	359	7.0	1.0	85.8
Spaghetti, raw	342	12.0	1.8	74.1
MISCELLANEOUS				
Curry powder	325	12.7	13.8	41.8
Peanut butter	623	22.6	53.7	13.1
Soy sauce	56	5.2	0.5	8.3

• INDEX •

Calcium mg	Iron mg	Sodium mg	Vitamin A (retinol) equivalent	Thiamin µg	Riboflavin mg	Niacin equivalent mg	Vitamin C mg
99	2.2	540	0	0.27	0.10	2.3	0
105	1.6	525	0	0.21	0.06	2.3	0
54	2.7	560	0	0.34	0.09	1.8	0
200	4.6	180	0	0.33	0.27	5.7	0
140	2.0	2	0	0.31	0.04	3.5	0
38	3.9	2	0	0.47	0.09	8.3	0
4	0.5	4	0	0.41	0.02	5.8	0
25	2.1	3	0	0.22	0.03	3.1	0
478	29.6	52	99	0.25	0.28	3.5	11
37	2.1	350	0	0.17	0.10	15	0
65	4.8	5,720	0	0.04	0.17	1.8	0